THE WORLD of THE UNSEEN

THE WORLD *of* THE UNSEEN

By

F. AMIR BAIYG'E

This is a work of creative nonfiction. The events are portrayed to the best of the author's memory. While all the stories in this book are true, some names and identifying details have been changed or withheld to protect the privacy of the people involved.

Copyright © 2019 F. Amir Baiyg'e

All rights reserved. No part of this book may be reproduced in any form or by any electronic or mechanical means, including information storage and retrieval systems, without permission in writing from the publisher, except by reviewers, who may quote brief passages in a review.

ISBN-13: 978-0692167793

ISBN-10: 069216779X

Library of Congress Control Number: 2018909290

Edited by: FirstEditing™ – USA

Designed by: Copy@ – Rosarito, B.C., México

Printed in United States of America

Published by: F. Amir Baiyg'e
P.O. Box 530690
San Diego, CA, 92153
E-mail: TheWorldoftheUnseen@gmail.com

TABLE OF CONTENTS

DEDICATION i
PREFACE iii
INTRODUCTION vii
PART 1 1
'The Jinnkind – The Scriptures – The Prophets' 1
   'References to the Jinn in the Glorious Quran' 3
   'The Honorable Prophet Solomon and the Jinn' 7
   'The Honorable Messiah Jesus Christ and the Jinn' 15
   'The Honorable Prophet Muhammad and the Jinn' 21
   'Prophet From Amongst You' 27
PART 2 33
'Cases of Jinn Possession' 33
   'The Woman with Cuts' 37
   'The Oppressed Couple' 41
   'The Black Dog Speaks' 43
   'The Black Dog Revisits – The Son of Sam' 47
   'The Devil Takes Over' 65
   'The Boy and the Quran' 71
   'Speaking Foreign Tongues' 75
   'Ibn Taymeeyah and the Jinn' 79
   'The Jinn Producing Items' 83
   'Ibn Hanbal and the Jinn' 87
   'The Jinn of Al-Uzza' 89
   'Stone Idol Drinks Milk' 93

PART 3 97

'Cases of Jinn Sightings and Jinn Activities' 97

'Jinn as Angels, Spirits, Ghosts, Psychics' 97

'The Jinn with Scroll from Prophet Solomon' 101

'Jinn Transporting Individuals to Arabia' 107

'Many Faced Jinn' 113

'Guard Sees Shape-Shifting Animal' 117

'Jinn Plaiting Horses' 119

'Jinn at the Presidential Palace' 123

'Jinn at American Military Base - The Story of Tamim Amini' ... 125

'The 29 Palms Jinn' 133

'Soldier Guards Border after Death' 139

'Spirit of Dead Brother' 147

'City Councilor Takes Photo of Spirit' 149

'I am Still Alive' 153

'Screaming From the Grave' 155

'The Jinn-Man Relations' 159

'The Ghost Lovers of Amethyst' 163

'The 100-Year-Old Ghost Lover' 167

'The Jinn or Dead Spirits' 171

'The Young Couple in Arizona' 174

'The Story of Shaykh Ahmad Izz ad-Deen' 176

'Amelie Van Tass Assisted by the Jinn' 183

'Government Use of Psychics' 187

PART 4 193

'Exorcism and Exorcists' 193

'Blowing the Holy Spirit' 195

'I Give You the Power' 197
PART 5 201
'Conclusion' 201

DEDICATION

To my teacher and mentor, the man who chose to become a father to me in woeful times, the extent of which is known only to me.

Safar M. Amir Baiyg'e

May the Almighty God give you the best in this World and the best in the Hereafter.

PREFACE

ALL OF THIS ACTUALLY OCCURRED! An unlettered woman suddenly begins speaking foreign languages. A dead man sings from his grave. A layman is transported thousands of miles away in minutes. And a President is forced out of his Presidential Office. All of this is the handiwork of those known in the Christian world as the Demons and in the Islamic world as the Jinn.

When I first heard of these true events taking place across the globe, naturally I was curious, always wanting more. I began researching and almost immediately became obsessed. All I could think about was the Jinn. Who are they? Why they do what they do? Can I speak with them? Will they speak with me? I always knew the Jinn existed. Growing up, I too had heard—like any other kid—the 'meant to scare' stories about the Jinn, which brought home even the wannabe tough kids shortly before sunset. Back then, I used to believe the Jinn lived in their own world, like a different planet. I assumed they lived on Mars or Jupiter. I would even place them farther out, way out, far beyond our galaxy. I guess back then I thought, the farther out I placed them, the safer I would be. Fast-forward to the year 2018: I am no longer a kid and I must face things, even those which I once feared.

Despite many warnings from religious leaders and my family and friends I decided to research and embark into the world of the Jinn. I recall my teacher saying to me, "Son, stay away from them for their world—despite being inter-linked with ours—is a dark and dangerous world." Another person told me something similar and I laughed but then he said, "By God, if you had seen what I have seen, you would not laugh." His tone was strange; it sent shivers up and down my spine. Nevertheless, I found myself reading books and articles that contained any information about the Jinn. I even read an ancient several-volume book without an index, or a glossary, or even a table of contents, which contained only a few scattered pages on the subject of the Jinn. I have read almost every book out there on the topic. I have read hundreds of articles written on Demonic or Jinn possessions in several languages. I have also spent hundreds of hours watching footage of exorcism sessions, Jinn activity and those that claim to be of Spirits, Ghosts and other beings. Interviews with people of knowledge, witnesses, and those possessed or formerly possessed took even longer. I travelled across the United States of America as well as Saudi Arabia, Afghanistan, and a few Central American nations in search of answers. I spent over a year in Mexico where stories about the Jinn or, as they are known in the Latin American nation, 'evil spirits' are widespread.

During my research I realized that the majority of books written about the Jinn were ancient and that the few books published in recent years contained therein verbatim information citing examples from the same ancient books, primarily the 13th century Islamic scholar Ibn Taymeeyah's magnum opus treatise on the Jinn. There is little to almost no reference to the activities of the Jinn occurring in our times. In the arguments to prove the existence of the Jinn, one must quote incidents of demonic possessions which took place hundreds of years ago during the lifetime of the great scholar Ibn Taymeeyah. My aim is not to change or update or even shed light on the works of the great scholars dealing with the world of the Jinn. Their works are scholarly and speak volumes. I am no scholar; I am not even the student of a student of a student of a scholar. I could add student many more times but I believe my point is clear.

The purpose of this book is to attempt to prove the existence of the Jinn via their more recent activities to the small group of people who still deny their existence on Earth yet advocate for spending enormous amounts of funds in the search for extraterrestrials a million light-years away.

The purpose of this book is not to spread fear but instead knowledge, as the Honorable Messiah stated,

"Seek ye the truth and the truth shall set you free."

And as the Honorable Prophet Muhammad stated,

"Seek knowledge from the cradle to the grave."

If through this book I achieve my purpose, then all praise is due to the Almighty God. And if I err, it is due to my own shortcomings.

F. Amir Baiyg'e - México

INTRODUCTION

IN ANCIENT TIMES, IF A MAN EXCELLED in a particular field, it was said of him, 'he is using his genius', or 'his genius is assisting him.' The ancient Latin word GEN-ius means the invisible spirit present with a man from the time of his birth. Similarly, the Arabic word Jinn simply means 'hidden from sight.' The words Djinn (Romanized) and Genie (Anglicized) both refer to the same being, commonly known in the Islamic world as the Jinn. Although the being known as the Jinn isn't new, the word (Jinn) has recently become popular in the English speaking world due to the Internet and movies, as well as war sightings reported by US and Allied soldiers from Iraq and Afghanistan of the beings known in the local areas as the Jinn.

The real Jinn, unlike the Aladdin character Genie of the Lamp, aren't cordial, cuddly, blue giants. However, like Aladdin's Genie they do often grant wishes, but, of course, not every wish, because the Jinn, like humans, are bound to certain limitations. The Jinn are created beings who live right here on Earth. They were its inhabitants long before Adam and Eve descended. One would be correct in describing the Jinn as the aboriginals of Earth. Although they do not recognize our land borders and man-made laws, they are constrained by the laws of the Almighty God. The Jinn have their own system of governance and leaders. Like Mankind, the Jinnkind also follow different religions. Amongst them are those who still follow the religion of Prophet Abraham and those who follow the Holy Scriptures of the Prophet-King Solomon and Prophet Moses. Many amongst them are followers of the Honorable Messiah Jesus Christ, and many more follow the religion of the Honorable Prophet Muhammad.

Amongst them are Jinn that are good and support Mankind. Also present amongst them are some Jinn that are evil and seek the destruction of Mankind. One might rightly ask why do the evil Jinns seek my destruction? Well, the enmity between Mankind and Jinnkind started a very long time ago, not on Earth but in the Heavens. This animosity comes from the time when their (Jinn) Father Satan refused to prostrate before our (Human) Father Adam. The enmity started the moment Satan refused to bow down to Adam and as a result was banished. The enmity continued when Satan whispered suggestions to Adam and Eve in the Garden, which in turn caused their banishment.

On Earth the offspring of Adam increased but so did the offspring of the Jinn, both good and evil. The animosity did not cease with the death of our Father Adam, and the children of Adam are not immune from it. In fact, the animosity is as bitter, if not more so, in our times as it was in the time of our Father.

A common misconception among some Christians and Muslims is that Satan was/is an Angel. Satan was not an Angel or a fallen Angel. Satan is from the Jinnkind. The evidence is clear. The Angels do not have free will, hence they cannot disobey any command of the Almighty God. They cannot do what they themselves want to do, but instead only those things they are commanded to do. Unlike the Angels, Mankind and Jinnkind have free will. It is due to the free will that Satan was able to disobey the command to prostrate before Adam. And it is due to the free will that Adam and Eve chose to believe Satan's whispers.

In the following pages, I will attempt to describe the evil Jinn and their more recent activities around the globe. They use different tactics but their goal is the same. Satan is destined to the fire, his final abode, and his desire is to take with him many from the descendants of his archenemy Adam.

The broadly held belief—mainly in the Western world—of Jinn being primarily an Arab or Islamic matter is pure fallacy. As we shall see in the following pages, the presence of the evil Jinn affects every human on Earth, regardless of his/her race, creed, or nationality. An American is not safe from them because he belongs to the mighty America, neither is an oil-rich Arab from the Arabian Peninsula nor an Afghan from the poor nation of Afghanistan. Only those with piety, who are God-conscious, are safe.

PART 1

'The Jinnkind – The Scriptures – The Prophets'

Almighty God created three, the Angel from pure light, the Jinn from smokeless fire, and the human from clay. The Almighty God granted free will to the Jinnkind and Mankind, but not to the Angels. The Angels, without free will, strictly follow the Divine Commands. Unlike the Angels, the Jinnkind and Mankind have the free will to decide whether or not to worship the Almighty God, as well as on worldly matters. Similar to Mankind, the Jinnkind have different communities with different leaders. They are males and females who produce children. They have different personalities, strength levels and temperaments. They follow different religions and some amongst them don't follow any religion. Amongst them are Jinn that are good and those that are evil. The Jinn eat and drink; they can walk, run or be stationary. Some Jinn even have the ability to fly in the air like birds. They live alone and with their families and tribes. They work and travel. The Jinn live much longer than humans, but they can age and do eventually die. And after death, in the Hereafter, they are rewarded or punished according to their deeds.

'References to the Jinn in the Glorious Quran'

The Jinn are mentioned by name in the Glorious Quran in several different chapters. In fact, the 72nd chapter of the Quran is titled 'Surah Al-Jinn' or Chapter of the Jinn. The very first verse of this chapter is sufficient as evidence of the existence of the Jinn amongst Humans.

It states,

"Say, [O Muhammad], it has been revealed to me that a group of the Jinn listened and said, 'indeed we have heard an amazing Quran [recitation]." **The Quran: Ch. 72 - V.1.**

There is a false belief amongst some people that the Earth was uninhabited before the descent of Adam and Eve. The Quran confirms that the Jinn inhabited Earth even before the creation of Adam and Eve. It states,

> *"And [mention, O Muhammad], when your Lord said to the Angels, 'Indeed, I will make upon the Earth a successive authority.' They said, 'will You place upon it one who causes corruption therein and sheds blood' . . ."* **The Quran: Ch. 2 - V. 30.**

In this verse, the Almighty God is saying to the Angels that He will create Adam, a human with free will. The Angels were aware of the earlier creation of the Almighty God, that of the Jinn, the being with free will. The Angels had also witnessed the Jinn causing corruption on Earth and this is what they referred to when they said 'will You place upon it [Earth], one who causes corruption therein.'

Furthermore, the Quran clearly states that the creation of the Jinnkind took place before the creation of Mankind. It states,

> *"And We did certainly create man out of clay from an*

altered black mud. And the Jinn We created before from scorching fire." **The Quran: Ch. 15 - V. 26-27.**

There are many other verses in the Glorious Quran regarding the Jinn, including verses confirming the existence of both good and evil Jinn as well as verses which indicate that the Day of Judgment and what comes after it are for both the Jinnkind and Mankind.

The Holy Gospel also contains passages regarding demons and demonic possessions. It also relates incidents where the Honorable Messiah performed exorcism on several possessed individuals, as we shall see in the following pages.

'The Honorable Prophet Solomon and the Jinn'

According to the Jews, Christians and Muslims, the Prophet-King Solomon was the son of Prophet David and one of the Prophets sent to the Children of Israel. Narrations differ over his rule as well as his piety and righteousness. Although Jews and Muslims agree that the Honorable Prophet Solomon had control over the supernatural beings, how he came to acquire that control varies.

According to the Hebrew Bible or the Old Testament, Prophet Solomon had 700 wives and 300 concubines. And some of his foreign wives turned him away from the worship of the Almighty God. Further, it claims Prophet Solomon built pagan shrines for the idols. It states,

"He [Solomon] had seven hundred wives of royal birth and three hundred concubines, and his wives led him astray. As Solomon grew old, his wives turned his heart after other gods, and his heart was not fully devoted to the Lord . . . He [Solomon] followed Ashtoreth, the goddess of the Sidonians, and Molek, the detestable god of the Ammonites. . . On a hill east of Jerusalem, Solomon built a high palace [temple] for Chemosh, the detestable god of Moab, and for Molek, the detestable god of the Ammonites. He [Solomon] did the same for all his foreign wives, who burned incense and offered sacrifices to their gods." **The Holy Bible: 1 Kings: Ch. 11 - V. 1-8.**

According to Rabbinical narrations written throughout Jewish history,

The Prophet Solomon prayed and asked the Almighty God for wisdom. The Almighty God answered his prayer and rewarded him with much more than wisdom. The Prophet Solomon was rewarded with riches as well as control over all the beasts, reptiles, spirits and demons. The Prophet Solomon was given a ring with the emblem commonly known as the Seal of Solomon, and he used this ring to rule over the demons. One day, a senior leader of the demons known as Asmodeus was captured and brought into the service of the Prophet Solomon. One day, the Prophet Solomon asked Asmodeus, 'What advantages do demons have over humans?' The leader of the demons Asmodeus responded, 'Give me your ring and unchain me so that I may demonstrate the advantages.' The Prophet Solomon unchained the demon and handed the ring to him. The demon Asmodeus took the ring and threw into the sea and a fish swallowed it. The demon Asmodeus then changed his form and turned into a large creature with wings. Asmodeus picked up Prophet Solomon and threw him 400 miles away, far outside the boundaries of his kingdom. The Prophet Solomon wandered around from city to city until he was captured in an Ammonite city and taken into captivity and forced to work in a kitchen. The Prophet Solomon worked in the kitchen and prepared food for the king of the Ammonites. Shortly afterwards, the king's daughter fell in love with the Prophet Solomon but the king disapproved of the relationship and ordered his soldiers to kill both of them by leaving them in the middle of the desert. The Prophet Solomon and the king's daughter roamed around the desert for a period of time until they reached a coastal city. Upon arrival at the coastal city, the Prophet Solomon immediately bought a fish so the two could eat. Miraculously, the Prophet Solomon bought the same exact fish that had swallowed his ring after it was thrown into the sea by the demon leader Asmodeus. Thankful at this miracle, the Prophet Solomon used his ring to once again rule as King over the kingdom and the demons, spirits, reptiles and beasts.

In regard to the use of and control over the supernatural, Rabbinical traditions from as early as the 1st century state,

"Prophet Solomon had an army of demons and once he dispatched the demon army to seek a virgin girl who had fled from him." **The Apocalypse of Adam.**

According to Jewish Rabbinical narrations, the Prophet Solomon built the Temple in Jerusalem. They claim that in building the Temple, the Prophet Solomon was helped by special mystical worms whose mere touch disintegrated large stones. The knowledge of this worm was given to the Prophet Solomon by the demon leader Asmodeus. They also claim the Prophet Solomon 'forced' some angels into helping him build the Temple.

There is little to no information regarding the Prophet Solomon or his rule over demons in the Holy Gospel. Christian writers and historians in recent times have accused the Honorable Prophet Solomon of practicing both white and black magic. Others state the Prophet Solomon used talismans and/or amulets to help individuals possessed by evil spirits or demons.

According to Islam, the Honorable Prophet Solomon was one of the mightiest Prophets of the Almighty God who ruled as King over the Children of Israel. He inherited the Kingdom and the Prophet-hood from his father Prophet David. The Glorious Quran states that the Almighty God bestowed many blessings on Prophet Solomon, such as command and control over the winds, birds and the Jinn. It states,

"And to David We gave Solomon [as a son]. An excellent servant, indeed he was one repeatedly turning back [to the Almighty God]." **The Quran: Ch. 38 - V. 30.**

"He [Solomon] said, 'my Lord, forgive me and grant me a kingdom such as will not belong to anyone after me. Indeed, You are the Bestower.' So We subjected to him the

wind blowing by his command, gently, wherever he directed, and [also] the devils [of the Jinn] – every builder and diver." **The Quran: Ch. 38 - V. 35-37.**

"And to Solomon [We subjected] the wind – its morning [journey was that of] a month – and its afternoon [journey was that of] a month, and We made flow for him a spring of [liquid] copper. And among the Jinn were those who worked for him by the permission of his Lord. . . . They made for him what he willed of elevated chambers, statues, bowls like reservoirs and stationary kettles. . . ." **The Quran: Ch. 34 - V 12-13.**

The Glorious Quran further states that the Prophet Solomon had an Army consisting of Mankind, Jinnkind and birds. It states,

"And Solomon inherited David. He [Solomon] said, 'O people, we have been taught the language of the birds, and we have been given from all things. Indeed this is evident bounty.' And gathered for Solomon were his soldiers of the Jinn and men and birds, and they were [marching] in rows." **The Quran: Ch. 27 - V. 16-17.**

It is further mentioned that the Jinn worked for Prophet Solomon until his death.

Unlike the Holy Bible, the Glorious Quran defends the honor, piety and righteousness of the Honorable Prophet Solomon. It states,

> "And We have certainly revealed to you [O Muhammad] verses [which are] clear proofs, and no one would deny them except the defiantly disobedient. Is it not [true] that every time they took a covenant a party of them threw it away? But, [in fact], most of them do not believe. And when a messenger from God came to them confirming that which was with them, a party of those who had been given the Scripture threw the Scripture of God behind their backs as if they did not know [what it contained]. And they followed [instead] what the devils had recited during the reign of Solomon. It was not Solomon who disbelieved, but the devils disbelieved, teaching people magic . . . But the Children of Israel certainly knew that whoever purchased the magic would not have in the Hereafter any share. And wretched is that for which they sold themselves, if they only knew. And if they had believed and feared God, then the reward from God would have

been [far] better, if they only knew." **The Quran: Ch. 2 - V. 99-102.**

'The Honorable Messiah Jesus Christ and the Jinn'

There are several references to the Jinn in the Holy Bible. There is sufficient evidence of evil Jinn and how they hurt humans by entering their bodies. In the Gospels, one can easily find instances where the Honorable Messiah Jesus Christ performed exorcism on individuals believed to be possessed by the Jinn. There is sufficient evidence in these stories to prove that the Jinn exist and that some amongst them are evil. And the act of exorcism in itself proves that the Jinn can and do enter the bodies of human beings. From amongst the four Gospels, the first three (Gospels of Matthew, Mark and Luke) each narrate incident(s) where the Messiah was witnessed performing exorcism on humans believed to be possessed by the Jinn. The only exception is the Gospel of John, which mentions no such incidents.

According to the Gospel of Matthew, one day during his Ministry, the Honorable Messiah decided to visit and to preach at the small village of Capernaum, located on the Northern shore of the Sea of Galilee. Shortly after arriving at the village, the Messiah began to preach to the different groups of people as well as perform healings and miracles. And as the night approached,

"many who were possessed by the demon were brought to him, and he drove out the spirits with a word and healed all the sick." **Gospel of Matthew: Ch. 8 - V. 16.**

Soon afterwards, the Messiah left the village of Capernaum and traveled to a village in the region of the Gadarenes when suddenly,

"two men possessed by the demon came from the tombs and met him. They were so violent that no one could pass that way. 'What do you want with us, son of God,' they shouted. 'Have you come here to punish us before the appointed time?'

There happened to be a large herd of pigs feeding in the distance. The demons begged Jesus, 'if you drive us out [then] send us into the herd of pigs.' Jesus said to them, 'Go!' They came out and went into the pigs, and the whole herd rushed down the steep bank into the lake and died in the water." **Gospel of Matthew: Ch. 8 - V. 28-32.**

According to the Gospel of Mark, one day, the Honorable Messiah while in the village of Capernaum walked into a Synagogue and began to preach. It was the Day of Sabbath and the Messiah was teaching the people when suddenly,

"a man in the Synagogue who was possessed by an evil spirit cried out, 'what do you want with us, Jesus of Nazareth? Have you come to destroy us? I know who you are – the Holy one of God!' Jesus said sternly, 'be quiet, come out of him!' Immediately, the evil spirit shook the man violently and came out of him with a shriek." **Gospel of Mark: Ch. 1 - V. 23-26.**

"That evening after sunset the people brought to Jesus all the sick and demon-possessed. The whole town gathered at the door, and Jesus healed many who had various diseases. He also drove out many demons, but he would not let the demons speak because they knew who he was." **Gospel of Mark: Ch. 1 - V. 32-34.**

The same story can also be found in the Gospel of Luke in Chapter 4, Verses 31-36, and 41.

According to the Gospel of Matthew, the Honorable Messiah performed a miracle by healing two blind men. The blind men became excited and despite the Messiah telling them not to, they notified the peoples of the town about this miracle. Shortly after the news of the miracle spread,

> *"a man who was possessed by the demon and could not speak was brought to Jesus. And when the demon was driven out, the man who had been mute spoke. The crowd was amazed and said 'nothing like this has ever been seen in Israel.'"*
Gospel of Matthew: Ch. 9 - V. 32-33.

These verses of the Holy Bible not only prove the existence of the Jinn but also the fact that demonic possessions have occurred throughout the history of mankind. These verses also show that the Jinn clearly knew the identity of the Honorable Messiah and that he only commanded the Jinn to leave the demented humans. There isn't any evidence suggesting that a particular verse of a Holy Book was used by the Honorable Messiah during the exorcism rituals. However, it must be understood that there is a significant difference between exorcism performed by a common man and that performed by the Messiah of God, as we shall see in the following pages.

I must note that there are remarkable similarities between the exorcisms performed by the Messiah and those performed by the Prophet Muhammad, as we shall see in the following pages.

'The Honorable Prophet Muhammad and the Jinn'

There are many narrations which confirm the Honorable Prophet Muhammad dealt with the Jinn on several occasions. The books of Hadith (Sayings and teachings of the Prophet Muhammad) confirm that the Jinn met with Prophet Muhammad on several occasions for various reasons. They state that during those meetings, the Prophet taught them the Quran and that many from amongst the Jinn accepted Islam. According to early Islamic books, the Jinn first met with the Honorable Prophet while he was in the Holy City of Makkah. In fact, the exact locations of those meetings are well-known.

Today there is mosque known as the Mosque of the Jinn, located a few minutes' walking distance from the Holiest site of Islam, the Holy Kab'ah. It is reported that the Jinn accepted Islam at the exact site where the Mosque of the Jinn stands today.

The books of Hadith state that many of the Companions of the Prophet witnessed him performing exorcisms on individuals possessed by the evil Jinn. There isn't any evidence suggesting that a particular verse of a Holy Book was used by Prophet Muhammad and the previous Prophets during exorcism rituals. It must be understood that there is a significant difference between exorcism performed by a common man and that performed by a Prophet of God. The Jinn are intelligent beings that are fully aware of their surroundings and if an exorcism happens to be taking place, the Jinn will know who he/she is dealing with; whether the exorcist is a common man or a Prophet of God or the Messiah of God. The common man may attempt to communicate with the Jinn to request him/her to leave the possessed human's body. The Christian priest reads out verses from the Holy Bible and the Muslim Imam recites verses from the Holy Quran. But when the exorcist is a chosen one of God such as the Honorable Messiah Jesus Christ or the

Honorable Prophet Muhammad, the exorcism is usually different. In the case of the Prophets performing exorcism, one can clearly see that the Prophets only command the Jinn to leave the body and as commanded, the Jinn departs without delay and again, this is because the Jinn are intelligent beings and aware of their surroundings.

There are some preserved authentic narrations regarding exorcism in the books of Hadith which show the similarities between the exorcisms performed by the Honorable Prophet Muhammad and those performed by the Honorable Messiah.

The Companion of the Honorable Prophet Muhammad, Ya'laa ibn Murrah, narrated that one day,

"I went on a journey with the Prophet, and as we were travelling on one of the roads, we passed by a woman who was sitting on the side of the road along with her young boy. This woman said, 'O Messenger of God, this child is overpowered by the Jinn several times a day. He is suffering and we are suffering because of him.' The Prophet was on his mount and said, 'give the boy to me.' As the boy was lifted, the Prophet placed him on his mount, directly in front himself. He held the

boy and opened his mouth and stated, 'O enemy of God, I am the Prophet of God, get out of him, get out of him.' The Prophet gave the boy back to the woman and said to her, 'meet me in the same place on our return journey to tell me how the boy has fared.' We continued on our way and later, on our return journey, we saw the same woman and her boy waiting. They had three sheep with them. The Prophet inquired about the health of the young boy and the woman stated, 'by the One God who sent you with the truth, we have not witnessed anything wrong with him so please take these sheep as a gift from us.' Then the Messenger of God ordered me to get off my mount and to take one sheep and return the rest to the woman." **Musnad of Imam Ahmad: Vo. 4 - H. 170.**

Here are some other narrations related to Jinn at the time of the Honorable Prophet Muhammad.

Another Companion of the Honorable Prophet Muhammad, Abdullah ibn Massoud, narrated that,

"One evening, we were in the company of the Prophet and then we missed him. After a while we began searching for him in the valleys and hills. We thought the Prophet had been taken away by the Jinn . . . . We spent the worst night that

people could ever have spent. Then at dawn, we saw the Prophet coming from the direction of [Mount] Hira. [We approached the Prophet and] we said, 'O Prophet, we missed you and we searched for you but we couldn't find you' ... The Prophet told us that 'there came to me a petitioner on behalf of the Jinn, so I went with him and recited the Quran to the Jinn'. ..." **Sahih of Imam Muslim.**

It is mentioned that the second Caliph of Islam, Umar Ibn al-Khattab, who was one of the closest Companions of the Honorable Prophet Muhammad, narrated,

"Once, a very old man [Jinn in the form of a man] came to meet with the Holy Prophet in [the blessed City of] Makkah. ... The Prophet asked him, 'tell me of your origin.' He responded, 'I am Haam, the son of Heem, the son of Lakhis, the son of Ibless.' The Prophet asked him for his age and he responded, 'I saw Qabil [Cain, the son of Adam] murder his brother Habil [Abel, the other son of Adam]. I was young, an adolescent at that time. I embraced the true faith of Abraham and witnessed his people throw him into the fire. I even tried to extinguish that fire. Then I embraced the true faith of Moses and Moses taught me of the Torah. Then I embraced the true faith of the Messiah and the Messiah taught me of the Gospel.'

Then he [the Jinn] said, 'O Prophet, I have a message for you.' The Prophet then asked him for the message. He responded, 'the Messiah said to me [that] after me, the Last Messenger would come to the world, and when you meet him, convey my greetings to him.' The Prophet felt very happy hearing this from Haam and thanked the Almighty God. Then the Prophet said, 'peace be unto you and my brother, the Messiah.' Then the Prophet asked Haam, 'do you need anything from me?' Haam responded, 'O Prophet, I want to embrace the true faith by your hand so teach me from the Quran.' The Prophet taught him ten chapters of the Quran. After that Haam disappeared and we never saw him again." **Al-Suyuti, Al Khasais-ul Kubra.**

I must note that although the above narration is recorded in several Islamic books written by pious scholars, some have questioned its validity and its chain of narrators.

'Prophet From Amongst You'

The Almighty God has stated in the Glorious Quran that He does not discipline a community until and unless they have been warned repeatedly by a Prophet from amongst themselves. The Jews, Christians and Muslims agree that the Almighty God has sent numerous human Prophets to mankind, but what about the Jinn? Were there Prophets sent to the Jinnkind? There isn't a straightforward answer to this question but there are signs in the Glorious Quran that suggest the Almighty God did send Jinn Prophets to the Jinnkind, as we shall see in the following pages.

It is stated in the Glorious Quran that,

"[Y]our Lord would not destroy the cities for wrongdoing while their people were unaware." **The Quran: Ch. 6 - V. 131.**

"And there was not a nation but that there passed within it a warner." **The Quran: Ch. 35 - V. 24.**

This verse clearly indicates that the Almighty God does not punish a community unless they have been warned repeatedly. And the Almighty God has sent Messengers and Prophets to all of the different communities of the world. This is confirmed by the Holy Bible as well as the Glorious Quran.

The books of Hadith (Sayings and teachings of the Honorable Prophet Muhammad) state,

"There were 124 thousand Prophets sent by the Almighty God." **Mishkat-ul Massabih: Vol. 3 – H. 5737.**

Furthermore, the Almighty God has provided the names of several communities and tribes to whom He had sent Prophets. In the Glorious Quran, the Almighty God states,

"And [O Muhammad], We have already sent messengers before you. Among them are those [whose stories]

THE WORLD of THE UNSEEN

We have related to you, and among them are those [whose stories] We have not related to you." **The Quran: Ch. 40 - V. 78.**

- *"And to [the tribe of] 'Aad [We sent] their brother Hud."*

  The Quran: Ch. 11 - V. 50.

- *"And to [the tribe of] Thamud [We sent] their brother Salih."*

  The Quran: Ch. 11 - V. 61.

- *"And to [the tribe of] Madyan [We sent] their brother Shu'ayb."*

  The Quran: Ch. 11 - V. 84.

- *"And We had certainly sent Noah to his people."*

  The Quran: Ch. 11 - V. 25.

- *"And indeed, Lot was from among the messengers."*

  The Quran: Ch. 37 - V. 133.

- *"And indeed, Elias was from among the messengers."*

  The Quran: Ch. 37 - V. 123.

- *"And indeed, Jonah was from among the messengers."*

  The Quran: Ch. 37 - V. 139.

- *"And We did certainly send Moses with Our signs and a clear authority."*

  The Quran: Ch. 11 - V. 96.

Even the Honorable Messiah Jesus Christ was sent to a particular tribe and this fact is confirmed by both the Holy Bible and the Glorious Quran. In the Holy Bible, the Honorable Messiah Jesus Christ states,

"Then Jesus said, 'I was not sent but unto the lost sheep of the house of Israel.'"

Gospel of Matthew: Ch. 15 - V 24.

The Almighty God confirms this statement in the Glorious Quran. The Almighty God states,

"And [the Almighty God made Jesus] a messenger to the Children of Israel."

The Quran: Ch. 3 - V.49.

"And We sent, following in their [the Prophets'] footsteps, Jesus, the son of Mary, confirming that which came before him in the Torah; and We gave him the Gospel . . ."

The Quran: Ch. 5 - V. 46.

We know that the last Messenger and Prophet of God was not only sent to Mankind, but also to the Jinnkind and everything else on Earth. Contrary to the beliefs of some minor groups, the majority of the people agree that the Honorable Prophet

Muhammad was commissioned as a Prophet of God to all the living creatures of Earth. In this regard, the Glorious Quran states,

"And We have not sent you, [O Muhammad], except as a mercy to the worlds [of humans, Jinns and all that exists]."

The Quran: Ch. 21 - V. 107.

All of the Holy verses listed above prove to us that indeed the Almighty God has sent Messengers and Prophets to all of the different communities of Mankind, Jinnkind and all other life forms that exist or existed on Earth, of whom we are not yet aware. Even today, in the year 2018, scientists are regularly discovering new creatures and life forms. We do not possess knowledge of all the life forms on Earth. The Almighty God states in the Glorious Quran,

"And mankind have not been given of knowledge except a little."

The Quran: Ch. 17 - V. 85.

And finally, the Glorious Quran mentions a community of Jinn on whom the Divine Punishment descended. And as we already know, the Divine Punishment does not descend on a community unless that community was repeatedly warned by Messengers and Prophets of God. The Glorious Quran states,

"[They say] 'Uff to you, do you promise me that I will be brought forth [from the Earth] when generations before me have already passed on [into oblivion]' . . . Woe be to you! Believe! Indeed, the promise of God is truth. But he says, 'this is not but legends of the former people' – Those are the ones upon whom the word has come into effect, [who will be] among nations which had passed on before them of Jinn and men. Indeed, they [all] were losers." **The Quran: Ch. 46 - V. 17-18.**

PART 2

'Cases of Jinn Possession'

Scholars of Judaism, Christianity and Islam agree that humans can be possessed. The evil Jinn occasionally possess men for various reasons, ranging from mere jest to revenge. In some cases the Jinn may possess a person after falling in love with him/her. Oftentimes, the Jinn possess a human body due to revenge, after some intentional/unintentional harm was done to the Jinn by the human. The evil Jinn may also possess a human solely to try and misguide other humans, and this trick of the evil Jinn has worked in the past and continues to misguide otherwise pious individuals. In the following pages, we shall see evidence of this trick of the evil Jinn. Oftentimes the Jinn may appear to an individual in the form of an animal or a human the individual recognizes and ask him to do certain things or whisper suggestions. The Jinn may also come to the residence of some individual or other places frequented by humans and commit an act to cause fear among the humans. This trick of the Jinn has worked in the past and continues to work even today, as we shall see in the following pages.

Oftentimes an individual possessed by the Jinn will do things that he/she couldn't possibly do or be capable of doing in a normal state. For instance, during the state of possession when the Jinn is controlling the body, the individual speaks in a foreign language or speaks in the opposite gender's voice. The individual may gain strength or literally become smart and read aloud an entire book from memory, as we shall see in the following pages.

In recent years, many people, whether common man or celebrity, have claimed to have been possessed or visited by the spirits, guardian angels, demons and/or the Jinn. Every day dozens of new videos of demonic possessions and exorcisms are uploaded on social media platforms. Many articles have been recently written on demonic possessions. Everyone claims that demonic possessions or the Jinn possession of the human body is on the rise.

Over 700 years ago, the great Islamic scholar Shaykh Ibn Taymeeyah wrote about the demonic possessions occurring during his own lifetime. Regarding the demonic possessions, Ibn Taymeeyah stated,

"If the veil were removed from the people of this time, we would find [that] most of the people of this time are possessed by the demons."

Some argue that if that was the case 700 years ago, what must be the case today when filth and corruption are widespread and Satan is worshipped openly in places like the 'Church of Satan' located in San Francisco, California and in many other places spread all across the United States, Europe and Asia. What must be our state when pornography is widespread and promoted on television shows and movies and even newspapers, when in every one second over 28 thousand people are watching porn videos, when in every 24 hours, 2.5 billion emails containing porn are sent and received, when every 98 seconds a person in the US is sexually assaulted, when every 40 seconds a person dies as a result of suicide. We mustn't be shocked if demonic possession is on the rise. When the human approaches filth, he walks away from the Almighty God, and when she is away from the Almighty God, the accursed Satan and his tribe of Jinn approach.

Recently, in the year 2018, the Vatican church opened its doors to train Bishops in exorcism due to the rise in the number of demonic possessions. One Priest from Sicily reported that the number of individuals possessed in Italy alone has tripled.

The International Association of Exorcists, which represents hundreds of Catholic, Anglican, and Orthodox Priests, stated that the increase in demonic possessions represents a 'Pastoral Emergency.'

'The Woman with Cuts'

It is widely believed that the Jinn inhabit and roam the valleys, deserts and abandoned areas far from human societies and civilizations. One such area is the valleys of Panjshir Province, Afghanistan. Behind the mesmerizing valleys and breathtaking mountainous views rests a great secret, mostly unknown to the outside world. It is often said that anyone who seeks the Jinn can find what he seeks in the Panjshir Valley. Panjshir is a mysterious area and even more mysterious are its tales relating to the Jinn and Jinn possessions.

In a distant corner of the valley, there lives a young married woman with her mother-in-law. It is said that the married woman was possessed by the Jinn, who would disturb and torment her. Eyewitnesses report that any attempts to communicate with the Jinn would often lead to bodily harm done to the possessed woman in the form of cuts appearing on her face.

The following is the eyewitness testimony of the mother-in-law, who stated,

"I would realize that my daughter-in-law is being possessed only after seeing her become angry without any reason. She would remain quiet and not speak with anyone nor respond to questions. She would take the clay pot and walk to the river to collect drinking water and not communicate with anyone. She would become angry and evil would be apparent on her face. I would understand that she is having another fit and I would take her into the room and close the door. I would then try to confront the Jinn by speaking in a soft tone, warning it [the Jinn] about the Hereafter and that oppressing an innocent woman would be justly dealt with in the Court of the Most High. While I would speak, my daughter-in-law and the Jinn in her body would remain silent and not respond, but the Jinn would become angry. Soon after the apparent anger, numerous cuts would appear on her face. The cuts would be

horizontal and about an inch in size. The cuts would be straight and sharp, as if cut by a razor blade, and would appear all over her face, including near the eyes and mouth. The cuts would remain on her face for about two days, after which all of the cuts would disappear, leaving no trace or marks on her face."

The mother-in-law recalls another incident which she witnessed along with other members of the family. She stated,

"I noticed that my daughter-in-law was having another fit and that the Jinn was disturbing her. As usual, I took her to the room and began speaking to the Jinn in her body. I said why are you disturbing her, aren't you afraid of the Almighty God? You torment her while she has done no harm to you, don't you fear the Almighty God? Instead of harassing her and cutting her face, why don't you do something good for her? Why don't you bring some fresh grapes for her so that she could eat them and heal! Why do you have to do harm to her? While I was saying these things, I heard a deep, strong voice which came from the mouth of my daughter-in-law but was not her own voice. The voice said, 'the grapes you requested are on the stairs outside the door.' Out of curiosity, I looked outside the door and saw fresh grapes just as it had been described. This happened sometime in the months of Jadi and Dalv

[Afghan months describing the time between December-February] when grapes are not in season and cannot be found in Panjshir Province or any of the surrounding Provinces."

As of the writing of this book, the woman is still alive and resides in Afghanistan. The Jinn continue to possess and torment her. The cuts continue to appear on her face.

In the ancient books, there are several stories describing events wherein the Jinn brought goods to humans from faraway places. One such story is mentioned by the great Islamic Scholar Ibn Taymeeyah, who narrates the story of Hussain al-Mansoor al-Hallaj, the man who claimed to be the personification of the Almighty God. It is stated,

"A group from the followers of al-Hallaj requested from him some sweets. He walked to a nearby place and then suddenly returned with a basket full of sweets. It was later discovered that the basket of sweets were stolen from the Yemen by the Jinn and brought to al-Hallaj [to give to his followers and continue his misguidance of being the personification of the Almighty God on Earth]."

'The Oppressed Couple'

There lives a family in Afghanistan who have been oppressed by the evil Jinn for several years. This pious married couple in Kabul City began having troubles over a decade ago and sought help in several different ways but nothing seemed to help. Many eyewitnesses testify to having seen this couple being oppressed by an unseen being. The relatives of the oppressed couple related this story.

"Shortly after the marriage took place, the wife began feeling a strange presence in her new house. Soon afterwards the husband felt the same. They witnessed unexplainable phenomena occurring at their small home, such as objects

moving and household items falling down and breaking. Then the wife began to have fits and she would shake rapidly and her voice would change. The Jinn began to oppress her and she was kept away from her husband. During an exorcism, the Jinn spoke and confirmed that she was being kept away from her husband. The Jinn would not disturb her as long as she remained in seclusion and away from her husband. But when the couple would try to have sexual relations or even get close to each other, the Jinn would harm her. It was terrible and there came a time that both were harmed only after speaking with each other. The couple were not allowed to speak, touch or even sleep in the same room with each other. On one occasion, the couple got together at night and slept together. When the husband woke up in the morning, he saw that his wife's head was partially shaved. This occurred several times and soon the wife's head was completely shaved. During another exorcism, the Jinn stated, 'as long as they keep away from each other, we will keep away from them.' The couple lived in the same house but apart from each other."

As of the writing of this book, the husband has passed away but the wife is still alive and the Jinn continue to possess her.

'The Black Dog Speaks'

During the lifetime of the 13th century Islamic Scholar Ibn Taymeeyah there lived a man who used to deal with black magic and the Jinn. This man was a Sufi master who dealt with the evil Jinn. The Jinn would do favors for him and he would in turn misguide others. The Jinn stole things for him and would oftentimes bring information to him about others. This man continued his ways for a long time.

Once he met with the great Shaykh Ibn Taymeeyah, he repented and changed his ways. He left his former ways and began to do good deeds. He began practicing orthodox Islam again. He then shared his story with Ibn Taymeeyah.

He stated,

> "*I used to walk around the streets of Damascus and a black poll with a light on top of it would lead the way for me. I also had had sex with women and young boys.*"

He then shared his personal interactions with the Jinn. He stated,

> "*I would be at a certain place and a black dog would come to me and converse with me. The black dog with white spots would say to me; '[This] person so and so has taken an oath by your name and he will come to you soon to inform you about it [and seek your help]. For your sake, I have already fulfilled the oath of that person.'*"

Once the black dog had left, the oath-taker would come to see the Sufi master as the Jinn had already stated. The Sufi master continued,

> "*Once the oath-taking person came to me, I would then notify him the details of his oath and give him the glad tidings of its fulfillment.*"

Shaykh Ibn Taymeeyah stated that once the Sufi master began

avoiding the forbidden deeds and kept away from his former ways, the black dog disappeared and he never saw it again.

'The Black Dog Revisits – The Son of Sam'

In the 1970s, a serial killer had terrorized the City of New York. This serial killer had caused widespread panic and fear amongst the residents of the city. People of New York were so afraid that most would not allow their children to leave their homes. Due to fear, women changed their dress codes and hairstyles to look different from the dead victims. They had seen pictures of the dead victims on the news channels, which covered the killings almost every day. This great panic led to the biggest man-hunt and police patrols in the history of New York. This is the story of the serial killer David Berkowitz, also known as the 'Son of Sam.'

A young couple in New York who couldn't have any children of their own decided to adopt a young boy. A young boy was located and the couple filled out all the legal paperwork. The young boy was taken home and named David Berkowitz. As a young child, David did not have many friends at school. He did not get along with the other students mostly due to his severe anger problems. David's anger problem was worrying his mother and she decided to take him to a child psychiatrist. After several sessions, the therapy was canceled due to David's unwillingness to open up to the psychiatrist. Despite his anger issues, David was very close to his mother and considered her as his only comforter and friend. David knew he was adopted and his adoptive parents had told him that his birth mother died giving birth to him and that his biological father had left them before that.

In the year 1966, following the Jewish tradition, David celebrated his Bar-Mitzvah. In the same year, a terrible event occurred which changed the young David forever. One early evening, David's mother prepared herself to attend a dinner party where her friends awaited her and as she walked out the front door, David yelled at her,

> "I hate you, mother, I hate you, I hate you. I hope you die."

THE WORLD *of* THE UNSEEN

That was the last time David saw his mother. She collapsed and died at the dinner party. David felt responsible and blamed himself for the death of his mother. She was buried at a nearby cemetery and David would often visit her.

David would walk for several hours around the cemetery, looking at tombstones and contemplating. He would mostly search for the tombstones with the names of girls, especially those who had died at a young age. For hours, David would think of these girls and wonder how they had died. He would ask himself, *'Were they pretty?'* David was always very close to his mother and had always considered her his only friend. After her death, he felt lonely and became depressed. He had no more friends.

In the year 1971, at the age of 18, David decided to join the United States Army. He wished to become a soldier and deploy to Vietnam to kill and become a war hero. He did join the US Army; however, he was not deployed to the battlefields of Vietnam, but instead to Korea, where he saw no battle.

In those days, it was common for prostitutes to linger outside the US military bases. Soldiers would often visit these brothels. David also attended these brothels and in fact, he even tried to make a prostitute his girlfriend but it did not work out well for him. It was after this failure that David started calling the prostitutes *'dirty'* and the act as a *'very disgraceful thing.'*

While deployed to Korea, David missed his deceased mother very much and would often think about her. He would blame himself for wishing her death. David thought he was responsible for the deaths of both his mothers, killing his birth mother by coming into this world and his adoptive mother by wishing her death. He hated himself and decided to write a letter to his father in New York. He wrote,

"Father, I apologize for being a burden and for amounting to nothing in society. I am sorry for turning out the way I did, stupid, hateful, ugly, and destructive. Forget me, I beg of you to forget that you ever had a son."

In the year 1973, the US Army transferred David to Fort Knox, Kentucky. Due to boredom, David joined a local Baptist church, which he frequently visited. He would attend the Sunday prayers and was soon thereafter baptized. At the church, David began reading the Holy Bible and was stunned to find therein verses pertaining to the fire of hell. He was scared because he blamed himself for the deaths of his mothers and also because he considered himself as unclean and evil. Immediately, he left the church, never to return again.

In the year 1974, David was given a discharge from the US Army due to several disciplinary actions. It is reported that David's Non-Commissioned Officers took disciplinary action against him on several occasions and as required wrote down his actions in the official Army forms. It is said that David was also given a US Army Article-15. This type of action is taken by the commander only after a serious misconduct. It is difficult to know what David's misconducts were for his records are not easily accessible. However, it is known that David received a discharge from the Army sometime in the year 1974.

In the same year, David returned to New York and shortly afterwards began attending school at the Bronx Community College. At around this time, David learned that his adoptive father, who had moved to the state of Florida, had re-married.

David became acquainted with his new family and immediately began hating his stepmother and stepsibling. David hated them and blamed them for taking away his father and ruining his relationship with him. At the same time, David began blaming himself for his father's new family. David said,

"There is a strong, dark presence which repels everyone around me." He began referring to himself as *"the dirty one."*

During this time, David met with an adoption movement group whose members were also mostly adopted and did not know their birth parents. The members of the group began asking questions about David's past. David told them what he had been told by his adoptive parents ever since he was a young boy. And that was that his birth mother had died during childbirth and that his biological father had left his mother before his birth. David recounted to the group that as a child, people made fun of him saying he killed his mother by coming into this world. David stated,

"People made fun of me and the kids at school taunted me saying, 'you killed your own mother.' When I was a child, I would have dreams wherein I would see my biological father

come to me and say 'I will kill you because you killed your mother.'"

A member of this group laughed at David, saying, *'This is what they tell all of us; they say our birth mother died during delivery and that our biological father had left long before that.'*

David was shocked and he immediately got in touch with his adoptive father in Florida and he began pressuring his father for the truth. His father finally told him the truth, that the adoption agency had told them not to share the identity of the biological parents.

After questioning, David found that his birth mother was alive and that his true birth name was 'Richard Falco.' David was shocked at this news but felt a relief because throughout his life, he had considered himself a murderer who had killed his own mother during childbirth. And now he knew the truth that his birth mother was still alive. David got hold of the adoption papers and found out the identities of his biological parents. He began searching for his birth mother but could not find a solid lead. He tried for several months without any luck.

At this point, David met with and joined a group of Satanists, a cult whose members believed in and worshipped and offered sacrifices to Satan. David fell in love with this cult and began to pray to Satan. He made a pact with Satan. David recalls,

"I chanted the names of Satan over and over and I kept calling on him and glorified him. I prayed, o my prince, o my lord, come into my life and take control of me. I felt as if I was being emptied out of my own personality and that something else was coming in to fill me."

The cult welcomed David as the newest member of the Satan family and he gladly accepted.

About a year or so after David had found the truth about his biological parents, he got lucky and found the phone number of his birth mother Betty. He called and spoke with her and after apologizing, Betty told David,

"On paper, your biological father is Tony Falco but he is not really your father. Tony Falco and I [Betty] were married and we had a daughter. Shortly after the birth of our daughter, Tony left me. I then had an affair with a wealthy Jewish businessman who was already married and had children of his own. From our affair, you were born and we

were ashamed to keep you because both of us were married to different people. We decided to give you up for adoption. Forgive me Richie, oh Richie, forgive me." [Richard or Richie was the birth name of David Berkowitz.]

David agreed to forgive his birth mother. He felt relief knowing that he had not killed his mother during childbirth as was told to him by his foster parents, which had disturbed him all of his life. Later, as David began thinking about his conversations with his birth mother Betty, his sigh of relief turned into anger. David wrote regarding his birth,

"Here I was, never wanting to be born in the first place, miserable, maladjusted, plagued with death fantasies, only to find out that I was unwanted, an accident after all!"

On a few occasions, David met with his step-sister and her family but those visits became shorter and shorter and then suddenly stopped. Regarding his family, David wrote,

"I was getting powerful urges [from the demon] to kill most of my family but I fought really hard to keep these urges from turning into actions. I just decided to stay away from them."

David's anger grew but he had decided not to hurt his own family so instead he decided to hurt someone else.

On Christmas Eve of 1975, David walked the streets of Bronx, New York, with a small pocket knife in hand. He saw a young girl walking the streets and he ran and attacked her with his knife. Fortunately, the young girl fought back hard and screamed loudly for help. She punched and kicked and finally managed to escape from David. David fled the scene and when he knew he was safe, he thought back about the attack. He did not regret hurting the young girl; instead, he decided to continue his spree but not with a knife. He decided to never use a knife again; instead he would use a gun.

In the year 1976, David was working as a security guard at a warehouse. He had been working at this job for over a year and during this time he mostly worked late night shifts. One night, David spoke to his manager and complained,

"I can no longer work night shifts because I have difficulty sleeping during the day due to the loud barking and howling of the dogs."

Shortly afterwards, David quit his warehouse job and moved out of his apartment because he kept hearing the barking of dogs. He moved to a new apartment but even there he continued to hear the barking and howling of dogs. During this time, David drove to Texas to meet with an ex-Army friend and while in Texas had his friend purchase a gun for him. With the handgun in his possession David returned to New York. While in New York, David continued to hear to howling of the dogs wherever he went. He decided that he had to sacrifice a woman's life in order to free himself of his torments. His demon would not let him be in peace so he began searching for a woman to sacrifice.

On July 29, 1976, David was driving in the Bronx searching for a 'sacrificial woman' when he saw two women sitting and talking inside a parked car. David drove past them and parked his car nearby. He then walked back toward the two girls and circled their car. Then David pulled out his gun and began shooting at the girls. David fired multiple times and then fled the scene. While fleeing the scene, David kept singing to himself. He felt a little peace because the howling of the dog had stopped and the demons were letting him be free for a moment. David was happy because the howling and barking of the dog had stopped momentarily. David later said,

> *"[Momentarily] I felt peace and after shooting them, I felt as if I was walking in the air."*

David read the newspaper the next day and became happy knowing that he had killed one of girls and critically injured the other. David was excited and began searching for his next sacrificial woman. Later in the same year, David shot and injured two other women and one man whom he had mistaken for a woman. He later wrote,

> *"I was passing the point after which a man plays and becomes God. I was anxious and excited and tense."*

On January 1977, David was driving around Queens, New York, searching for his next sacrificial target when he saw a young woman and a man sitting inside a parked car. David approached them and began shooting the girl. He killed the girl but the man was left unharmed.

On March 8, 1977, David was once again in Queens, New York, when he saw a young girl walking in the street with several books in her hand. David immediately cut her off and started to walk toward her from the opposite direction. As they walked near each other, David pulled out his gun and pointed it toward the girl. It was dark outside and as the girl approached David, she saw the gun pointed toward her face. David shot her in the head without any hesitation.

By this time the New York Police Department had realized that a serial killer was out on the streets. The Police Department put out public alerts and began calling David 'the .44 [Caliber] Killer.' Panic and fear spread like wildfire amongst the public. Women began to cut short and change their hairstyle and most dyed their hair different colors, avoiding black. They feared that the killer was out killing women with long black hair.

After his military discharge, when David had returned to New York, he had changed apartments a few times. In one of the last residences, David had a neighbor by the name of Mr. Sam Carr. Mr. Carr had a black dog that he called Harvey. According to the other neighbors, the black dog Harvey was a normal protection dog like any other. It seemed like no one had any issues with the animal, with the sole exception of David, the .44 Caliber Killer. David would hear [probably imaginary] the dog howling and barking non-stop. This disturbed him very much and David wrote multiple letters to the owner of the dog but received no response. In the final letter to the dog's owner, David wrote,

> *"I told you how the barking and wheezing and howling [of your dog Harvey] was destroying my digestion and my family [David lived alone, he probably meant imaginary family]. How the barking and the howling would make me scream, scream out begging for the noise to stop. It never stopped. . . . My life is destroyed now. I have nothing to lose. I can see that there shall be no peace in my life until I end yours. . . . I have called out the names of the masters: John Wheaties, General Jack Cosmo, the Womb Raider. Their verdict is unanimous. You are dead . . . I will see you in hell. . . ."*

A few days after the letter was sent, David walked to the back yard of Mr. Carr's house and shot dead his black dog Harvey.

David's killings had terrified the city. The newspapers of New York such as the Daily News placed an ad-type appeal in their own newspaper and literally begged 'the .44 [Caliber] Killer' to turn himself in to the authorities. In response, David wrote a letter to the Daily News. He wrote,

> *"Hello from the gutters of New York City, which are filled with dog manure, vomit, stale wine, urine, and blood. Hello from the sewers of New York City . . . You can forget about me if you like because I don't care for publicity. However, you must not forget about Donna Lauria [a victim] and you cannot let the people forget her, either. She was a sweet girl but Sam is a thirsty lad and he won't let me stop killing until he gets his fill of blood. . . . Do not think that because you haven't heard from me for a while that I went to sleep. No, rather, I am still here. Like a spirit roaming the night. Thirsty, hungry, seldom stopping to rest; anxious to please Sam! I love my work. Now, the void has been filled."*

On June 26, 1977, David attacked another couple outside a club and injured them but both survived. With each murder, David was becoming happier, satisfying his demons, and the people of New York were becoming more terrified. On July 29, 1977, exactly a year after the death of Miss Donna Lauria, who was David's first deceased victim, the newspapers began publishing articles with titles such as 'tell us what is next for us, Son of Sam.' Before the arrival of the July 29, 1977 anniversary, David had written to the Daily News and the Police Department warning them that he would kill again on the anniversary.

Everyone was waiting and expecting another kill but David did not kill. He terrorized the public and it was a lie. David would not kill on the anniversary; instead, he would kill two days later. This made for even more headlines and newspapers throughout the world began publishing articles about 'the .44 [Caliber] killer', 'the Son of Sam.'

On July 31, 1977, David attacked another couple who were sitting inside their car. One was injured and the other proclaimed dead. This unfortunate death made headlines throughout the world and every news outlet covered the story.

A few weeks later via a parking ticket, the New York Police Department apprehended David along with his .44 Caliber weapon. The Son of Sam was in custody and hundreds and thousands of cameramen and journalists surrounded the Police Department. All of the footage available shows the Son of Sam smiling, with no remorse what-so-ever.

Immediately after his apprehension, the police officials questioned the Son of Sam and asked why he had killed. His initial response was, *'It was a demon who told me to kill.'* The

Son of Sam was then transferred to a psychiatrist for an evaluation. During the tape-recorded evaluation the doctor asks, *'David, why did you do it?'* He responds,

"I had nothing against these victims. Who were these people to me? They were just people. I didn't hate them. I wasn't angry against them. Sam did it through me. He used me. He made me go out there and do it. I did it for him, for blood."

During his captivity and trial, the Son of Sam claimed that he had gotten into Satan worship and that he was often visited by the Demons.

The Son of Sam finally stated,

"The black dog would come to me and command me to kill. It was Sam who told me to kill and Sam is the Demon."

'The Devil Takes Over'

On February 20, 2016, a series of shootings occurred in and around the County of Kalamazoo, Michigan. By early next morning, the Police Department identified Jason Brian Dalton as the shooter. The 45-year-old Jason Dalton, an Uber taxi driver by profession, lived a normal life with his wife and children. Jason had no criminal record and was described as a decent family man.

On February 20, 2016, shortly after 4:00 p.m., Jason Dalton received an Uber taxi pick-up request on his phone, which he accepted. Moments later, Jason arrived at the pick-up location where the customer was waiting for the Uber taxi to take him to a nearby location. The customer recalls,

> *"During the trip, he [Jason] received a phone call after which he began to drive crazy. He ignored the stop signs, entered into oncoming traffic lanes and [sideswiped] another vehicle. I pleaded with him to stop the car and when he came to a stop at a stop sign, I jumped out of the car and contacted the police."*

At around 5:15 p.m., Jason received another Uber taxi pick-up request on his phone, which he accepted. Shortly afterwards, Jason arrived at a parking lot and saw a woman. He asked the lady if she was so-and-so [the customer waiting for Uber] and she responded in the negative. Later she stated,

> *"A man in a vehicle with a German Shepherd type dog in the back seat confronted me and asked if I was this person by a different name. I responded no, and he pulled out a gun and began to shoot at me several times. I survived by acting dead."*

Later, the police concluded that 15 shots were fired at the woman who was in the parking lot, along with her daughter and several other children.

At around 10:01 p.m., Jason appeared at a nearby car dealership where he approached two men who were standing and talking among themselves. According to the witnesses,

> "After parking his car, he [Jason] approached the two men, who were father and son, and confronted them, saying 'What are you looking at?' Before they could answer, Jason pulled out his gun and began shooting at them."

It was later concluded that Jason shot altogether 18 rounds at the two men, killing both instantly.

At around 10:30 p.m., Jason appeared in the parking lot of a restaurant where he saw a woman inside a van. Jason approached the woman and began shooting at her. A witness later stated,

> "After shooting the woman, Jason turned toward the adjacent two vehicles wherein four people were sitting. He began shooting at them and then fled the scene."

It was later concluded that at this location, Jason killed four people and seriously wounded another. The witnesses contacted the Police Department and provided the description of Jason as well as his vehicle information. About two hours after the final incident, police officers apprehended Jason with the crime weapon still in his possession.

After the initial investigation, the police concluded that the victims were not related and the shootings appeared to be random. Since then several detectives have questioned Jason, as well as psychiatrists and other court officials. The police report states that during the initial and follow-up questionings,

"Jason Danton acknowledged that he recognized the Uber [taxi] symbol as being that of the Eastern Star, and a devil head popped up on his screen, and when he pressed the button on the app, that is when all the problems started."

"Danton told us that literally, when he logged onto [the Uber app], it started making him be like a puppet, [the devil head] would give you an assignment and it would literally take over your whole body."

"Danton said he wishes he would never have spoken what that symbol was when he saw it on his phone. Danton described the devil figure as a horned cow head...and then it would give you an assignment and it would literally take over your whole body."

"Danton told the police that he did not drink or smoke, and was not on psychotic or psychosis drugs, adding that he

was not in bad financial straits and did not consider himself an anti-government or militia type person."

Jason Danton stated, *'He is not a killer'* but *'knows that he has killed.'*

'The Boy and the Quran'

Imam Hassan Ali is a well-known Muslim Imam in the United Kingdom. A few years ago, he gave a lecture on the world of the Jinn and during the lecture, he recounted an incident which he had witnessed as an adolescent. In the 1990s, a large group of Muslim students were being taught the Glorious Quran and the head-teacher needed a large location to accommodate the students. An abandoned Royal Air Force building was located somewhere in Nottingham, UK, and the head-teacher moved his students to the building. The following story was witnessed by dozens of individuals.

Imam Hassan Ali stated,

"We moved into the building and it was a massive building with 120 rooms, divided into west and east wings. The teacher placed us in a few rooms of the east wing and warned us not to go to the west wing of the building. We were kids and a group of us dared each other to go to the west wing, at around 12 o' clock in the afternoon, in broad daylight. As we were walking [in the west wing] . . . we heard doors banging and screeching . . . and we ran back to the east wing. [In the group of students was] a young 13-year-old kid from Bangladesh who did not know a word of English [and only spoke Bengali] . . . and he was the quietest kid you could imagine . . . and he was trying to become a Hafiz of Quran [to memorize the entire Quran] and he had memorized only one Juzz [which is 1 of 30 parts of the Quran]. So one day . . . he strays off and goes to the other side [to the west wing] and [then later] he comes back . . . to his teacher and puts the Quran in front of his teacher and says 'TEST ME' . . . in Arabic [language]. This kid suddenly knew Arabic. The teacher looked at him and just laughed . . . [but the kid insisted saying] test me, test me, [from] anywhere you want. So the teacher said okay . . . read from the 15th Juzz . . . [and the boy read from memory the 15th Juzz of the Quran in Arabic without any sort of accent]. The teacher then tested him from another place [of the Quran] and then another and *then another. This kid now [suddenly] knew the [entire] Quran [by heart]. And the kid [began to] challenge the teacher in speaking Arabic [and the eloquence of the Arabic language]. This kid had really good Arabic [skills] all of a sudden. . . . [Then one day] he takes a clipper and shaves half of his head and leaves the other half as it is. . . . "*

Imam Hassan Ali states that the teacher realized the boy was possessed by the Jinn and began performing an exorcism on him. The Imam was present during the exorcism and states that the teacher would recite verses from the Glorious Quran and the possessing Jinn in the body of the 13-year-old boy would recite counter-verses from the Glorious Quran. For instance, the teacher would recite verses warning the Jinn of Hellfire and the Jinn would recite verses regarding Paradise. The teacher concluded that the boy was possessed by a Jinn belonging to a group of traveling Jinns who were temporarily staying in the massive building. The teacher ordered that the boy be taken back to his hometown and left there for a period of one month, after which the Jinn would voluntarily leave the boy to rejoin the group of Jinns. The boy was taken to his home where he continued to act differently. However, after about a month, the Jinn left the boy and he became better again. After the Jinn had departed, the boy became normal, the same as he was: quiet, shy, kept to himself, and only knew one Juzz of the Quran and had no Arabic language skills.

'Speaking Foreign Tongues'

In the highly informative book titled, *'The Exorcist Tradition in Islam'*, the author Dr. Bilal Philips writes about seven different exorcists and their stories and experiences. During the interviews, amongst other questions, Dr. Philips asks the exorcists about their encounters with the Jinn who spoke in foreign languages. A Muslim Egyptian exorcist by the name of Shaykh Muhammad Taahir Abdul-Muhsin described his personal experience dealing with the Jinn who spoke in a language alien to the possessed human.

Shaykh Muhammad Taahir Abdul-Muhsin stated,

> *"We found a [male Urdu speaking] Jinn in an Egyptian*

[Arabic speaking] woman. . . . [The Jinn] was originally from Pakistan. He said that he was on Hajj and fell in love with her and returned with her to Egypt. . . . [In Urdu] he said that he lived in an abandoned apartment and that he had over ten thousand children and grandchildren. Some people may hear this and ask, 'how could ten thousand live in one apartment?' However, we already pointed out that they may take the form of vermin, like ants."

"I also helped a Saudi [man] married to an Egyptian woman who used to curse her husband in different languages, like English and French. I communicated with the Jinn in Arabic, and it left her after promising to do so."

A similar incident occurred more recently in the Panjshir Valley of Afghanistan. A 60-year-old unlettered woman who had lived in a small village in Panjshir Valley all of her life suddenly became possessed by the Jinn. The old woman only knew one language, Dari, her mother's tongue. She had never had any schooling. Eyewitnesses described to me that sometime in the year 2009,

"The old woman became possessed by the Jinn. She

was sitting with us in a group and suddenly started shaking very rapidly and her relatives began holding her down. The old woman disliked it and began speaking to her relatives and the watchers in English and Pashto. Then she started to read out loud the numerals in English, saying one, two, three! We called in a local religious man who recited verses from the Quran and the old woman got better."

The elderly woman is still alive and resides in the same village in Panjshir Valley, Afghanistan. The Jinn continue to possess her.

Yet another case of Jinn possession was reported by the Economist, the well-known English language magazine. The correspondent for the Economist travelled to the Panjshir Valley of Afghanistan and interviewed some former bodyguards of the deceased Northern Alliance commander Ahmad Shah Massoud. During the interview, the guards stated,

"The cook had been possessed by a Jinn the week before. He was a devout man . . . a non-smoker and illiterate. He fell ill. When he recovered, he found he could speak and

write in many languages. The Jinn that was in him was well-travelled but also pushy. It [the Jinn] demanded a cigarette, then another, and then it became impatient and swallowed lighted cigarettes whole."

'Ibn Taymeeyah and the Jinn'

The Shaykh of Islam, Ahmad Ibn Abdul-Haleem Ibn Taymeeyah, was one of the greatest Islamic Scholars of history. Ibn Taymeeyah was born in the year 1263CE in ancient Northern Iraq, the son and grandson of great Muslim scholars. During his life, Ibn Taymeeyah wrote several books and gave many rulings. His work has been relied upon throughout history by scholars, theologians and historians of various religions. Ibn Taymeeyah's work has had great effect, even on the scholars of our times. Amongst his students are the world-renowned Ibn al-Qayeem and Ibn Katheer, the man who wrote a several-volume book literally covering everything from the beginning of times up until his own time and also the Day of Reckoning and what may come beyond.

Ibn al-Qayeem, one of the students of the great Shaykh, recalls the encounters of his teacher with the Jinn and the many times he performed exorcisms. Ibn al-Qayeem states,

"My teacher Ibn Taymeeyah would often perform exorcism rituals on individuals possessed by the Jinn. During those exorcism rituals, he would use several different verses of the Holy Quran. There was one particular verse from the Holy Quran which he would recite on all of the possessed individuals. This was the 115th verse of the 23rd Chapter of the Holy Quran which he would recite in the ear of the possessed person."

"Did you [Jinnkind and Mankind] think [that] We created you in play and that you would not return to Us?" **The Quran: Ch. 23 - V. 115.**

Ibn al-Qayeem recalls that the great Shaykh Ibn Taymeeyah told him about a particular occasion when he was performing an exorcism ritual on a possessed person.

"My teacher Ibn Taymeeyah was performing exorcism

on a mad-man and during the ritual, he read in the ear of the mad-man, 'Did you think that We created you in play and that you would not return to Us?' Immediately the Jinn said in a drawn-out voice 'yesssssss!' My teacher started to beat the mad-man [the Jinn in the body of the mad-man] on his neck with a stick, until the people present had thought that the mad-man had died. Immediately the Jinn began speaking loudly and said, 'but I love him.' My teacher responded saying, 'he doesn't love you.' The Jinn said, 'I want to go to Hajj with him', my teacher responded, 'he doesn't want to go to Hajj with you.' The Jinn continued saying, 'okay, I shall leave him for your sake', and my teacher responded, 'no, but do leave in obedience to the Almighty God and His Messenger.' The Jinn agreed and said, 'okay, then I will leave him.' Immediately the mad-man stood up and looking around suspiciously, he asked 'why am I in the presence of the honorable Shaykh?' The people present were amused and jokingly asked, 'and what about all the beating that you received?' He responded by questioning, 'for what crime would the honorable Shaykh beat me?' The mad-man had not felt the beating [for the beating falls on the Jinn]."

'The Jinn Producing Items'

In the ancient books, there are several narrations regarding the Jinn and their ability to produce items in a split second. In his books, the great Islamic Scholar Ibn Taymeeyah mentions a man present during his own time to whom the Jinn brought sweets from faraway places. He also mentions a similar story about another man to whom the Jinn brought whatever he wished.

Ibn Taymeeyah states,

"There lived a Shaykh who was intelligent and knowledgeable in the religious science and the Quran. The evil Jinn came to him and eventually managed to trick and seduce

him. The Jinn told him that the mandatory prayers were no longer required of him [due to his righteousness, wisdom and piousness]. The Jinn told him that they would bring him anything his heart desired. When the Shaykh fell for the deception and complied, the Jinn began to bring him fruits and sweets and other things. This process continued until the religious scholars advised him that he had been deceived by the Jinn. Once the Shaykh repented, the Jinn stopped visiting."

Another similar incident occurred more recently. A very reliable eye-witness reported to me that,

"Our family had gathered and we were sitting in a small room when suddenly this person so and so, who is a family member, started acting differently. This person's voice and tone changed and we realized that the Jinn had possessed him. We began to speak with the possessed person and asked the Jinn to leave. During the conversation, in a terrible voice, the Jinn stated, 'I have recently returned from performing Hajj.' A family member who was skeptical stated, 'well, then why didn't you bring us some Holy Water from the ZamZam well or some Arabian dates?' We were holding the arms of the possessed person when suddenly he said, 'leave my arms.' The possessed person appeared calm so we complied. The

possessed person then moved his hands behind his back and then placed them in front of him. Lo and behold, there were large date fruits in his hands. There was one date fruit for each person in the room, and no more and no less. Due to fear, we took the dates but everyone remained silent afterwards."

'Ibn Hanbal and the Jinn'

It is narrated in the history books as well as some ancient religious books that in the Baghdad Court of the 9th century Islamic Caliphate, a female servant became possessed by the Jinn. The Caliph Al-Mutawakkil sent word of the demonic possession to the great Muslim scholar Imam Ahmad Ibn Hanbal. The great Imam sent one of his students to the Court of the Caliph with a plain message to the possessing Jinn.

The message of Imam Ahmad Ibn Hanbal said,

"In the Name of the Almighty God, Ahmad says it is not permissible for you [the Jinn] to possess this woman's body,

and Ahmad commands you to depart from this woman's body." Then, in the presence of the Caliph and his advisors, the Jinn possessing the female servant responded in a male's voice. The Jinn said,

"Ahmad's command is welcome for Ahmad is one of those who obey the Almighty God and the Almighty God has made everything obedient of Ahmad. If Ahmad ordered us to leave Iraq, we would certainly do so."

With that, the male Jinn departed from the body of the female servant and she became better.

'The Jinn of Al-Uzza'

Muslims under the leadership of the Honorable Prophet Muhammad were numerous and the Command came from the Almighty God for the conquest of the Holy City of Makkah. The Honorable Prophet entered Makkah without any major resistance. At the time there were about 360 different idols in and around the Holy Kab'ah. The Honorable Prophet smashed and destroyed all of the false gods who were worshiped at the Holy Site.

Shortly after the conquest of Makkah, the Honorable Prophet issued an important mission to his companion Khalid Bin Al-Waleed. Khalid was to travel to a town known as Nakhla and destroy the idol of the goddess Al-Uzza. This goddess was one of the main idols of the polytheists.

As commanded, Khalid took thirty Muslim soldiers under his command and traveled to Nakhla. Apparently, at that time there were two Nakhlas, a Nakhla valley and a nearby Nakhla town. Khalid went to the Nakhla valley first and found therein a normal appearing idol and he smashed it into pieces. Excited at the completion of his mission, Khalid returned to Makkah and reported to the Honorable Prophet, who asked him, *'Did you see anything unusual while you destroyed the idol?'* *'No'*, replied Khalid. *'Then you have not destroyed Al-Uzza; return to it'*, said the Honorable Prophet.

Khalid, now angry at his previous mistake, traveled to the correct Nakhla town but this time he would not return without accomplishing his mission. Khalid entered the sanctuary within Nakhla town and saw therein a black-skinned woman with long, disheveled hair standing in his way. She was naked and kept wailing. Khalid realized it was an evil Jinn which used to possess the idol of Al-Uzza. Without hesitation, Khalid drew his sword and cut her [the Jinn] in two pieces. Khalid returned to the Honorable Prophet and recounted what he had just seen. The Honorable Prophet responded saying, *'That was indeed Al-Uzza and she will never again be worshipped in this land.'*

'Stone Idol Drinks Milk'

On September 21, 1995, before dawn, a holy man in New Delhi, India walks into the shrine to perform his daily ritual which includes prayers and offering milk to the idol. The idol is the Hindu elephant-headed god Ganesha. The man is a bit tired and sleepy but continues with the ritual. Everything seems ordinary and the man fills the small silver bowl with milk and walks close to the idol. He places the milk bowl near the trunk or mouth of the idol and suddenly the milk starts to flow upwards and disappear out of the bowl. The idol Ganesha has just drunk milk.

The man rushes out of the shrine and sees that it's still dark outside. He doesn't waste a minute and walks hurriedly to the house of the local priest, Radha Krishna Bharadwaj. He knocks at the door, yelling, *'Pandit Ji, Pandit Ji'* which means Priest. *'Lord Ganesha is drinking milk, Lord Ganesha is drinking milk,'* says the man, trying to get the Priest to come witness the miracle. The Priest rushes to the shrine, where the man hands over a bowl of milk to him. He takes some milk in a spoon and bends forward slightly and places the spoonful of milk near mouth of the idol. He is shocked to see the milk flowing out of the spoon and into the trunk of the elephant-headed idol. *'Lord Ganesha drank milk; it is a miracle,'* says the priest in a loud voice. Moments later, the people of the neighborhood gather outside the shrine to witness the miracle and get blessings, each person carrying a bowl of milk in one hand and a spoon in the other. As the dawn approached so did the local news cameras which recorded the miracle and showed it on television causing a media outbreak. Soon major news stations like the CNN and BBC captured the story and broadcast it around the world.

Priests from all corners of India started reporting a similar phenomenon occurring inside their shrines. A major social services organization known as the Vishva Hindu Parishad, which provides relief to Hindus across the world, announced that *'a miracle was occurring.'*

At the same time, Hindu shrines all across the globe were reporting similar miracles. Hindu shrines in Canada, Nepal, United Kingdom, and United Arab Emirates as well as others started reporting similar miracles occurring at their shrines. In the United States of America, several people reported witnessing the milk-drinking miracle at the Hindu Temple Society of North America, also known as the Lord Ganesha Temple.

It is reported that at some shrines the line of people waiting to offer milk to the idol stretched as far as two kilometers. Hundreds of thousands of people took to the streets to celebrate the miracle. The event brought India to a standstill. The Government of India started an immediate investigation by dispatching Mr. Ross McDowall of the Ministry of Science and Technology to one of the Temples where the alleged miracle was occurring. Mr. McDowall offered a spoonful of milk to the idol and again the milk started disappearing from the spoon. The Government began searching for a scientific explanation and several were provided to debunk the miracle. But to the

Hindus who worship the elephant-headed idol Ganesha, further confirmation of the miracle happened when at the evening of that day, the idols stopped drinking milk.

About ten years later, on August 21, 2006, news of a similar milk-drinking idol miracle was reported in the City of Bareilly, Uttar Pradesh. Shortly afterwards, other temples across India reported similar miracles.

PART 3

'Cases of Jinn Sightings and Jinn Activities'

'Jinn as Angels, Spirits, Ghosts, Psychics'

The Jinn can appear to a human and whisper suggestions or provide him with some physical thing or with information. Oftentimes, the evil Jinn will do this to try and misguide the individual and, through him/her, other innocent people. The Jinn may appear to an individual in the form of an animal or a human the individual recognizes. The evil Jinn may also take the form of a bright, beautiful being and claim to be an Angel of the Almighty God. There have been several reported cases of the Jinn claiming to be Angels and transporting individuals from one location to another location far away in a very short period of time. Many such cases have been recorded where the Jinn have appeared to humans and have claimed to be an Angel or a Soul/Spirit of a deceased family member. The Jinn may also appear and have sexual relations with humans. The Jinn may lie and claim to be the spirit of so and so or a ghost lover and have sexual relations with a person. Many times, the evil Jinn may force themselves upon a human and have unwanted sexual relations. Such cases are numerous and have been recorded throughout known history by scholars of different religions. The evil Jinn may also appear in a scary devilish form and attempt to scare an individual and cause fear amongst humans. This could be a mere joke on the part of the Jinn or a smokescreen for other evil intentions. In the following pages, we shall see such cases of Jinn sightings. Many individuals have come forward claiming to be able to speak with dead spirits and many more claim to have a special psychic ability. These cases are numerous and in each one of them, the Jinnkind are involved who play tricks on mankind, as we shall see in the following pages.

Muslim scholars agree that the Jinn are a sort of shape-shifters who may take several forms and appear to humans. The Jinn can take the form of an animal or a bird or a human. It must be understood that humans cannot see the Jinn in their original form, the way they were created by the Almighty God. Renowned Muslim scholars concur that mankind are not able to see the Jinnkind in their original form and the sole exception to this reality are the Prophets of the Almighty God. The scholars agree that throughout history mankind has encountered the Jinnkind but only when the Jinn appeared in the form of a human, animal, bird, beast, etc.

The renowned 8th century Islamic scholar Imam Al-Shafi'i, as well as the 11th century Islamic scholar Imam Al-Bayhaqi, stated that,

"We shall invalidate the statement of any individual who claims to have seen the Jinn, except the Prophets of the Almighty God."

The 14th century Islamic scholar Imam Al-Asqalani commented on this famous ruling and stated,

"The statement of Imam Al-Shafi'i only applies to those individuals who claim to have seen the Jinnkind in their original form—the form Almighty God created them in—and not the forms the Jinnkind normally take, like that of an animal or a human."

The Glorious Quran confirms this and the Almighty God states,

"Indeed, Satan and his tribe [of Jinn] see you from where you do not see them." **The Quran: Ch. 7 - V. 27.**

The following pages contain cases of Jinn sightings as well as other Jinn activities to include causing fear and misconception and having sexual intercourse with humans amongst other things. Some of these cases were witnessed by several individuals and others were narrated to me by eyewitnesses or those with firsthand knowledge of the incidents.

'The Jinn with Scroll from Prophet Solomon'

This extremely unique story comes from the ancient land of knowledge, the City of Kabul, Afghanistan. The person transmitting this story is my noble teacher who relates the strange phenomenon which occurred to his own spiritual teacher and Shaykh, a very just religious leader and a devout servant of the Almighty God, who has now passed, may the Almighty God have mercy on him.

The Shaykh related this incident to my teacher. He stated,
"I was at a gathering with the grand Imam and some

religious scholars of Kabul when unexpectedly a local resident approached the Imam and began to complain. This resident stated, 'dear Imam, I am a farmer with a few acres of land in such-and-such place. Naturally, I tend to my land and plant crops for this is my livelihood. There is a corner portion of my land that every time I try to walk, something which I cannot see attempts to scare me and prevents me from going to it. Several strange things have occurred to me at this place. I am hoping that you would travel with me to my land and help me.' The Imam looked toward me and said, 'Shaykh; would you travel with the brother to his land and see what is causing him difficulty?' I agreed and shortly afterwards traveled with the troubled farmer to his lands. We arrived together at the land and there were no buildings nearby. There were no lights visible anywhere and the night was very dark. We walked to a certain point at the land and the farmer suddenly stopped. He handed me a lamp and pointed me toward a location and said, 'I cannot go beyond this point; this is the point after which they await.' I asked him who he was referring to but he couldn't give me a commonsensical answer. I left him there and continued walking toward the location with the burning lamp in my hand. Once I felt I was approaching the area described to me, I started praying. I prayed in my heart and then out loud. I recited verses from the Holy Quran and then began questioning. I said, In the Name of the Almighty God, who are you and what do you want? Show yourself to me. Suddenly from out of nowhere, a shape emerged from the ground up. It was as if a person was on the ground that slowly arose to stand upright. It took the shape of a man but not a normal man, instead several times larger than a man—like a giant but not evil-looking nor unsympathetic. I stared up toward what seemed like his face and questioned him again. Immediately he responded in a human-type voice saying, 'As-sallam-u Alaykum.' I responded to his greetings of peace and then asked him for the third time who he was and what he was doing here. He responded saying, 'this is my property, this is my land.' I corrected him saying this land belongs to the farmer who has inherited it from his father, and for that reason, you [the being] have no right to be on it without explicit permission. He spoke again and said, 'I have the valid right to this land which was given to me by the one who had authority.' I asked him for proof and he said, 'please see me here tomorrow evening and I shall produce for you evidence that should suffice.' I agreed and departed from the area. On my way back, I saw the farmer waiting impatiently. He asked questions but I told him to have patience and that I would return again the following evening.

I left and as arranged, returned the following evening. I walked to the same location and the being appeared just as he had the previous evening. Again, he greeted me saying, 'As-sallam-u Alaykum' and I responded to his greetings of peace. He then handed me an old parchment scroll. It was a large scroll which I unrolled and began reviewing. The document had visible writings on it and a corner of it was marked. It was a stamp which appeared to be the seal of the Prophet Solomon. I questioned him regarding the parchment scroll and he said, 'Sufficient for me is the Almighty God as witness, this document is my evidence that this land was given to me by the Prophet of the Almighty God, Solomon.' I handed the parchment scroll back to him and greeted him. He walked away and disappeared and I walked back to the other side of the land. There I saw the farmer waiting who appeared very nervous [for he had seen the being that was communicating with me]. I advised him to leave that portion of the land and not to travel to it or farm it and in return no harm would befall him. He agreed and was satisfied."

Another unrelated but similar phenomenon was witnessed by a United States Special Forces team deployed to Afghanistan in the year 2002. Some allegedly leaked military reports as well as interviews show that a Special Forces team was operating in the Kandahar Province when suddenly, *'the communications stopped working and it appeared as if something was interfering with it.'* Shortly afterwards, loud shrieks were heard which put fear in the hearts of the seasoned warriors. Out of fear the team took cover near a cave and took their battle positions. Then in broad daylight, the team encountered a giant being, *'several times larger than a man.'* The Special Forces team fired hundreds of bullets at the giant being but could not harm it.

Recently, a video emerged online which appears to show a being which looks like a human but several times larger, like a giant. The leaker of this footage is believed to be a former member of the US military. The footage shows scenes of an active battle in an unknown location inside Afghanistan, where helicopters are firing ammunition rounds at and around what seems to be a giant being. It is believed that the scene was captured sometime in the year 2002 or 2007.

The United States government officials usually ignore these claims and never discuss them. The government doesn't give any attention to such claims and they usually fade away before any sort of scrutiny or investigation. Due to this, the common man usually concludes that since the government isn't talking about it, it is of no importance and/or false.

However, according to several individuals and online sites, when the rumors came out regarding the encounter with a giant being in Afghanistan, the United States Department of Defense issued a statement which in part stated that the US has no information about any giants in Afghanistan.

Some skeptics have questioned the US military's recent use of the Massive Ordinance Air Blast (MOAB) or Mother of All Bombs in Afghanistan. In April 2017, the US military dropped an eleven-ton bomb on Nangarhar Province of Afghanistan. The twenty-one-thousand-pound bomb dropped near a mountain is the largest non-nuclear conventional bomb ever used. Some have questioned who the logical target of the bomb could be, if not the giant beings who appear and disappear into thin air in Afghanistan.

'Jinn Transporting Individuals to Arabia'

Throughout history, countless cases have been recorded of individuals who were transported by the Jinn from a certain place to a nearby village, or to a far-away city and even to a different country, thousands of miles away. Such cases have been reported by historians and religious philosophers of all times, as well as common folk who wrote down their personal 'Jinn-Transportation' experiences.

One such story comes from the Holy Land of Jerusalem, Palestine, whence a man would be seen by his relatives standing in Makkah, Saudi Arabia during the day, only to be seen by his family in Palestine in the evening of the same day. This occurred at a time when horses and camels were the primary mode of transportation and automobiles had not been produced.

The story is as follows,

"There lived an old man in Palestine who made his righteousness and piety known to the people. The old man would perform good deeds in plain view of the people and the people took him for a saint. People respected him and considered him to be a man of God. Every year, during the season of Hajj, hundreds of pilgrims would leave Palestine for Makkah, Saudi Arabia to perform the Hajj rituals. The journey would take about a month and the people would leave a month before the beginning of the Hajj so that they didn't miss the Hajj season. Once the pilgrims had arrived at Makkah, Saudi Arabia, the old man, who would still be present in Palestine, would begin to collect gifts and letters from the families of the pilgrims. When all the letters and gifts were in his possession, he would walk toward the desert and then disappear into thin air. Early the next morning, the old man would be present in Makkah handing out the letters and gifts to those to whom they belonged. Once the gifts and letters were handed out, the man would walk toward the desert and disappear again. By the next day, the old man would re-appear in Palestine claiming that all had gone well. When death was approaching the old man, he called for his oldest son and told him the following,

'Son, when I die, go to the desert in such-and-such place and you will find therein a camel and you will know what to do.'

After the burial of his father, the boy walked toward the area his late father had told him. Once he reached there, he saw a normal looking camel but the camel began to speak with him in a human-type voice. The camel said to him,

'Your father used to prostrate to me; he worshiped me and in return, I would do for him favors which you already know about.'

The boy understood that the camel was an evil Jinn [in the form of a camel] and he refused to bow down and worship it. The camel continued insisting but the boy stood firm. Shortly afterwards, the camel ran away and disappeared, never to be seen again. The boy returned to his village where he told everyone the truth about his late father and the devil he used to worship."

I personally know another man who resides in Northern California who claims to have been transported to Makkah, Saudi Arabia on several occasions. Although I am quite familiar with this man, I do not believe it is right to mention his name or provide his identity here in this book. The man is fairly wealthy and is in no need of money, proving that he is not falsifying for any financial gains. He is highly educated in the worldly sense of the word but not so much in religious studies. Neither his parents, nor siblings or spouse or children have any mental disorder. In fact, I know his children and they are highly educated and decent folks. In reality, the man has not been to Hajj or Saudi Arabia the way I and millions of other Muslims have but he is able to describe the environment surrounding the Holy Mosque with details that only a person who had been there would know. He claims to have been transported to Makkah, Saudi Arabia by an angelic being that only he can see. The last such transportation occurred somewhere in the year 2015.

The man stated to me,

> *"I was sitting at home when the being [described to me as an Angel but in reality, an evil one from the Jinn] came and told me to perform ablution, which I did. He then asked me to*

walk outside my house to an open area, which I did. Once I was outside, the being lifted me in the air, not by his hands, but instead by a word. The being flew me to Makkah [to so and so location] in the vicinity of the Kab'ah. Once I laid eyes upon the Kab'ah, I stopped flying but I was still in the air. I noticed a few stairway-type white steps which were about ten and descending. I could see thousands of people circumambulating the Kab'ah. At this time, I was still in the air but not flying toward any particular direction. I was only observing and as I observed, the crowd of people circumambulating and everyone else froze in their spot. It was as if someone had pressed the pause button on a remote control. Suddenly, my clothes changed and I was wearing the white robes [Ihram]. Then as the other people stood silent in the spots, I flew toward the Kab'ah and began circumambulating it. When I completed the seven circuits, I flew back to the top of the stairs and turned around to face the Kab'ah one last time. I stood in the air for a short while and then flew back outside the Holy Mosque. From there, I flew back to the open area near my house [in Northern California]. The distance takes an airplane about 20 hours but the [Angelic] being transports me in a few short moments."

Several such cases have been recorded by Muslim scholars

throughout history. The great Islamic Shaykh Ibn Taymeeyah in his books relates the story of a man who dealt with the evil Jinn and that the Jinn would transport him from the mountains to nearby villages in and around Damascus.

'Many Faced Jinn'

There are numerous recorded cases of people claiming to have seen the Jinn in various forms such as dogs, birds and other animals. There are also stories in ancient books which state that the devil can take different forms and change forms. Over the years, several cases have been recorded where an individual saw a person who he recognized but then suddenly the person's face changed or the person completely disappeared into thin air. I know a person that currently lives in the State of Arizona, United States, who witnessed a similar strange phenomenon. This person is reliable and I am personally acquainted with him. He stated,

"In the year 1994, I was a young boy and we lived in

Maimana City of Afghanistan. One late evening, I was sitting by the window of the second-floor bedroom, facing the front road. There was no electricity that evening and candles were lit nearby. I was looking out the window, watching and waiting for my brother-in-law to come home from work. I was told to announce his arrival so that my family could walk downstairs and open the door for him. Moments later, I saw a human figure in the distance walking toward our house, and I assumed it was my brother-in-law. I was not sure so I waited for the figure to get closer before announcing the arrival. When the figure got closer to a clear visible distance, I saw it to be my brother-in-law walking toward our house. I announced it, saying, 'he is here.' But then the face of the figure changed and it became an old woman. I simply thought I had made a mistake so I announced again, saying, 'it is not him, but an old woman.' Seconds later, as I stared at it, the face changed again and became that of my brother-in-law. Then I saw my brother-in-law look up toward me as he smiled and waved. Naturally, I also waved but as I was waving, I saw the figure change form and turn into an old woman. It kept changing faces even as I stared at it. The fear shook me to my core and I froze. I wanted to speak but I was scared. I realized I had seen a Jinn and as I turned my head to tell my family, something happened and I fainted. When I woke up, my family was gathered around me. Hours later, my brother-in-law came and when questioned, he stated that he was not in the neighborhood at the time when I saw his face in the figure."

In the ancient books, there are many similar stories regarding the Jinn taking the form of an individual, whether dead or alive, and one such story is recorded by the great Islamic Shaykh Ibn Taymeeyah. The Shaykh says about himself,

"I know of many such instances where people have called upon me during difficulty and calamities. I know a person who was afraid of the Romans and when confronted [by the Romans] called out to me for help. Suddenly the same person saw me in the air and I repelled his enemy for him."

Ibn Taymeeyah states, 'I informed the person that I did not hear his cries nor did I help defeat his enemy for him, and that it was the evil Jinn that had taken my form to misguide him after he had called on other than the Almighty God. . . .'

'Guard Sees Shape-Shifting Animal'

In the year 2005, a former Army soldier was hired by an influential family to guard them and their residence, located in Karachi City of Pakistan. A seasoned soldier, he always carried with him a shotgun. One late night, a strange phenomenon occurred that changed the seasoned warrior forever. He saw a shape-shifting Jinn. For several days, the soldier continued telling the same story to the family over and over again. The guard stated,

"It was a silent night except that the occasional howling of the stray dogs could be heard. I was at my post outside the house, carrying my shotgun in my hand. Then my

eyes fell upon a rabbit that kept moving in a dark area across the street from me. As I stared at it, the rabbit suddenly looked back toward me. Moments later, the rabbit started coming toward me. Then suddenly the rabbit's shape changed and it turned into a cat and began making sounds. I became very scared and held on to my shotgun. Until that moment, I thought I was hallucinating or that it was just an illusion. Then the cat began to take the shape of a half-woman. At that moment, I don't know how but I screamed out of fear and began to walk away from it. That is when you [the family] heard my screams. . . ."

The family stated that after the incident, the former soldier's behavior changed and he was never the same person again.

'Jinn Plaiting Horses'

There are numerous reports of Jinn disturbing humans which have been recorded throughout history but rarely do we hear of a Jinn that harasses animals. This is one rare story which occurred in the old Kabul City of Afghanistan in the 1960s. I personally know the person relating this story. He is a former senior government official and is deeply involved in religious studies. From an early age, he studied religion under one of the most leading religious figures of Afghanistan. He currently resides in California and recounted the story of his deceased mother. He stated,

"My mother was old and she suffered from chronic pain. At night, while everyone else slept, she would sit by the window and contemplate because the pain would not allow her any sleep. During one such night whilst looking out the window she noticed something strange which she later described to us as 'a Jinn abusing the horse.'"

My mother stated,

> 'It was very late at night. I was sitting by the window when suddenly the horse started whinnying. The horse continued whinnying loudly and there was no one near the animal. Moments later the horse's hair began lifting as if someone was holding up its mane but again there was no human around. The horse's whinnying increased and it looked scared. Then the horse's mane started turning into plaits. There was an unseen being playing with the horse's mane and plaiting [braiding] it. When the plait was complete, it would slowly unplait. I could see the plait being undone. This process continued throughout the night and it only stopped once the early morning call-to-prayer was heard. When day approached, sweat was visible on the horse's body. The horse sweated so much that is seemed as if someone had poured buckets of water over it.'

"My mother witnessed the same strange phenomenon on several nights and each time she related the story to our family." This occurred in Afghanistan sometime in the 1960s.

The same incident occurred again 49 years later, but this time in the United Kingdom, in the year 2009. The Police Department in the City of Dorset, England responded to a distressed call by a farmer who complained that his horses had been plaited and maltreated.

The farm owner told the investigators,

"One of my horse's manes was plaited [and] it took me sometime to unpick it and the wind had whipped it into a sort of dreadlock, but underneath were three strands neatly plaited. It is most bizarre. Whatever it is there, there is a lot of fear and anxiety. I know of about 12 other horses that have had it [plait] done."

The same strange phenomenon also occurred at other nearby farms. After investigation and speaking with those practicing witchcraft, the Police Department concluded that it appeared to be part of a ritual where the knots [plaiting] are used to cast a spell on someone.

'Jinn at the Presidential Palace'

In March 2017, the Brazilian President Michel Temer and his family evacuated their official residence at the Alvorada Presidential Palace due to disturbances by evil spirits and/or ghosts. This sudden and unexpected move from the Presidential Palace raised questions and the President was forced to issue a public statement and give an interview.

"I wasn't able to sleep", said the President, who is a devout Catholic. *"I felt something strange there."* The President wasn't alone; his wife, the First Lady Marcela Temer, also felt a strange presence at the Presidential Palace. The President and his family believed that there was an evil spirit at

the Presidential Palace haunting them. And after a few tormented nights, the President contacted a Priest who specialized in exorcism and asked him to help drive out the evil spirits.

As such, the Catholic exorcist was secretly brought into the Alvorada Presidential Palace where he performed rituals to get rid of the evil spirits. Despite the exorcism rituals, the President and his family continued to feel the presence of 'evil spirits' and wondered if it were 'ghosts' haunting them. When the exorcism did not work, the President along with his family left the Alvorada Presidential Palace and moved into the Vice Presidential Residence.

'Jinn at American Military Base - The Story of Tamim Amini'

Post 9/11, the United States federal government began assigning troops to different regions of the world for its Global War on Terrorism. With the War on Terrorism being fought mostly in Afghanistan, the US soldiers were sent in thousands to specific military installations across the continental United States to complete a new and specific type of training known as the pre-deployment training, which can be up to eight weeks in duration. During this time, the soldier learns about the culture, religion and history of Afghanistan as well as the day-to-day life of an Afghan. Every effort is made to make the pre-deployment training as realistic as possible. To achieve this, the United States military has built a 'base' within the military base. For the remainder of this story, we shall call this 'base' within the base 'the Afghan village.' Millions of dollars have been spent on the Afghan village to make it appear like an actual village of Afghanistan. There are houses of mud and clay as well as those made of shipping containers. There is a mosque and the call to prayer (the Adh'an) can be heard from it five times a day during the actual prayer times. Hundreds of Afghan-Americans are contracted by the US military who act as 'role players' and each is given a specific role to play during the eight-week long training course. A mayor is chosen from amongst them as well as an Afghan Army commander, a doctor, a farmer and so on. About a dozen men are chosen to act as 'Op-4' meaning Opposition Forces or in other words, terrorists and enemy combatants. The Afghan role players who are now the residents of the Afghan village speak only in Dari and/or Pashto languages. They dress in native Afghan clothing and eat Afghan dishes and converse amongst each other in the native language. During the training, soldiers are sent on patrols and during the patrols, the Op-4 carries out ambushes. Often, the Op-4 carries out offensive operations wherein they carry out attacks on the soldiers while they are sleeping or

THE WORLD *of* THE UNSEEN

visiting the Afghan village. As mentioned previously, every effort has been taken to make the pre-deployment training as realistic as possible, to give the soldiers a taste of Afghanistan and what they could expect from their upcoming deployment, hence preparing them for changes about to come. These US military training bases are usually very far out of the cities and residential areas.

One such base in the Mojave Desert of California is known as the NTC or the National Training Center in Fort Irwin. Fort Irwin is a major US military installation and has its own Afghan village where thousands of soldiers receive their pre-deployment training in the vast abandoned desert.

In May of the year 2013, a new group of US soldiers were sent to the Mojave Desert for training and as usual, the Afghan village was prepped and each villager was assigned a role he/she would play for the next eight weeks. Most of the villagers had had over three years of experience at the same job. They had participated in dozens of such courses. The villagers knew each other and every night after the training had ended, they would sit together and share experiences. One man by the name of Tamim Amini had worked at this vast Mojave Desert for over four years, role-playing and training the US soldiers. He was a common face at the Afghan village and one of the first role players at this military base. Tamim's role was that of an Afghan police chief, commanding a stimulated police station in a distant corner of the desert. His job was to assist the in-training US soldiers in their patrols. He would stay at the police station for several hours at a time and often during the night with a few other role players.

It was during one such training when a few of the role players started complaining to Tamim about seeing shadows, hearing voices and other unexplainable phenomenon. Tamim disregarded them at first but after more people came forward, he started to take notice. Tamim recalled one man who complained to him, saying, *"I hear a voice calling for me and when I turn toward the direction of the voice, it fades."* To calm the man, Tamim told him, *"It must be one of our guys pulling a prank on you,"* but he was not the only man complaining, recalled Tamim. Another man complained that someone came up behind him and breathed on his neck; he stated, *"I felt the warm air on the back of my neck which made me scream and I did not have the power to even turn around;*

THE WORLD *of* THE UNSEEN

instead, I ran in the direction I was facing." The man was so pale, recalled Tamim, *"he quit his job after describing the events to me, and no one could convince him to stay."* At night, when all trainings had ended, the villagers would gather on the roof of a container-house and share stories, sing songs and recite poetry. *"But lately, the stories were about ghosts, spirits, and the Jinn,"* recalled Tamim.

Tamim states that although he believes in the existence of the Jinn, he did not believe his colleagues to be telling the truth, mostly due to the elders amongst them denouncing their claims and making fun of them. *"I guess it is easier to say they are lying than to accept it as the truth and remain fearful,"* added Tamim. The complaints increased and it became harder and harder to ignore them. Then one day something happened that changed everyone's perception of the events.

"On the second week of July 2013, after a 48-hour long training mission, we came back to our container-barracks completely worn out. No one amongst us had had any sleep. We were dusty, hungry and tired and all we wanted to do was to sleep," recalled Tamim, as he nervously moved side-to-side

on his chair relating this story to me. *"Everyone went to his assigned military bunk inside the door-less containers, which are stacked horizontally on both sides with a hallway in the middle, dividing the male and female sleep quarters, and at the end of the hallway are two bathrooms across from each other. A loud voice reminding everyone to 'shut up' and 'let us all sleep'"* was the last thing heard before Tamim's eyes could not remain open anymore and he fell asleep. *"Only God knows how long I slept,"* recalled Tamim, when suddenly *"I heard an extremely loud but scary scream of a man which shook me to my core and I jumped up out of my bunk, shaking and unable to move, and with my heart pounding. I could not dare take a step outside my container from where the voices were coming. The situation of my colleagues was no different and we were alert and the word sleep had left our minds."* Tamim's first thought was, *"I am alive and unhurt"* and it was only then that he was able to walk outside the container. *"Less than 10 feet away from me was my colleague Bashir, down on the hallway floor, sliding and pulling himself toward the exit. Bashir was pale, gasping for air and trying to say something but his words were broken, and he was unable to stand on his feet and was instead crawling and dragging his body away, while his eyes were locked toward one of the rooms on the female side of the hallway. I took a step or two towards Bashir,"* recalled Tamim. *"I looked to my left and saw a girl levitating. She was lying on her bed and her body would rise up about two feet, with her legs bent slightly and her thick hair down. I began praying and saying, 'I seek refugee with God' and those around me were also humming prayers rapidly. We saw the body rise from the bed more than four times and each time the body moved up and down in a split second."* The body of the possessed girl would rise from the bed so rapidly that Tamim thought the bones were broken. *"It appeared as if someone had placed his hands under the waist of the girl and was lifting her up very rapidly,"* recalled Tamim. *"Some of the people who saw the girl began screaming and others ran outside the building, yet others were helping Bashir."*

Tamim stated he was one of the last persons to run outside the building. *"Not a single a person amongst us had the courage to stay and watch,"* recalled Tamim, as the hair on his arms bristled, even now as he related the story to me, two years after its occurrence. According to Tamim, US Army medics were called to the scene to examine the girl.

'The 29 Palms Jinn'

Marine Corps Air Ground Combat Center, simply known as 'the 29 Palms Base', is the largest military installation of the Marine Corps in the continental United States. I have personally visited the 29 Palms Base on several occasions and like anyone else who has been around this base will tell you, it is large—a vast open desert with harsh terrain and very scary. It is not for the faint-hearted. The 29 Palms Base is mostly a desert with no civilization nearby and its stories of ghost and spirit sightings are well known amongst the United States marines and soldiers.

Some foreign language experts are also contracted to support the marines and soldiers in their training exercises such as the pre-deployment training. I am acquainted with several of these civilians who have related to me their personal encounters with the Jinn, while supporting the training exercises at the 29 Palms Base. I am also well-acquainted with many US military personnel who have personally witnessed several strange phenomena while training in the desert of the 29 Palms Base.

Recently, a US marine wrote of his personal encounters with the Jinn while training at the 29 Palms military base.

He wrote,

"To put things in perspective as to how far away we are from civilization, the closest manmade object is a three-hour ride away. This day was particularly hot . . . so we spent all day hiding under camouflage netting, getting classes about various military tactics. Once the sun set, we set off into the night to get some hard realistic training done. . . . The sky is absolutely cluttered with stars. I can see a shooting star every few seconds. . . . Finally, after roaming around aimlessly for what felt like forever, we head back and we're granted a few hours of sleep. I lay down and start to drift off. [Then] I am suddenly woken up [for watch duty] after what felt like 10

minutes and I get up instantly. . . . I get dressed and I stand my post dutifully like I'm told at the checkpoint. I'm given a radio and told to only lift the barbwire after it gets approved over the radio. It's maybe around 2am and everyone else in my company is dead asleep except for myself and an officer in the comm [communications] truck. All I can hear are the coyotes. I decide to start looking at the stars with my night vision [goggles]. I hear a coyote yelp off in the distance and think nothing of it. A few moments later, another marine comes over a small hill in front [of] me. Nothing crazy, probably [out to answer the call of nature] . . . He walks toward me but his eyes don't really reflect light. Rationally, one of us is probably dehydrated so I think nothing of it.

He approaches me and after a few seconds of staring at me, he simply says,

'Can I come in?'

His voice didn't sound right. [There was] no inflection or questioning tone. Weird!

I ask him what his name was and why he was out so far . . . [to answer the call of nature].

He tells me his name, 'Sergeant Wright', and he ignores . . . [the second part of my question]. Same weird voice! Granted,

I'm new to the unit so I don't know anyone named Sergeant Wright but I still had to verify it.

[So I radioed in], Main, this is Roadguard 1. Main, this is Roadguard 1. There is a Sergeant Wright requesting entry. Over.

[Over the radio, I get a response from the soldier at the communications truck],

'Roadguard 1, this is Main. There is no Sergeant Wright in this company and the closest unit [to you] is 25 miles away. Make sure . . . get the f... back here right now. Don't let him in or [don't] even look at him. Run.'

As the weird dude started to hear this, his face changed to severely angry. Like he wanted to rip my throat out and drink my blood. By the time I got back, everyone is awake. All of the vehicle lights are turned on and everyone is packing up, scrambling into the trucks. We leave . . . and drive the entire three hours back. I never got an explanation from anyone but my squad leader who was a simple, backwoods kind of guy, bluntly said [to me] that whatever I saw wasn't asking to get through the gate."

The marine later figured out that it was a Demon or a Jinn

playing with him and asking for permission to enter and possess his body when it asked, 'Can I come in?'

'Soldier Guards Border after Death'

It was cold and dark, an unusual moonless night providing perfect cover to the company of the Indian Army soldiers maneuvering against their enemy, the People's Liberation Army of China. This is the India-China war of 1962. A dispute at the Himalayan border erupts into a full war between the militaries of India and China in a region known as Aksai Chin by the latter and Jammu Kashmir by the former. On or about the year 1959, the massive Chinese Government intervention in Tibet causes the Tibetan Uprising. In response, the Indian government takes a series of calculated steps, the first of which grants asylum to the Dalai Lama, followed by the Indian Forward Policy initiative, which paved the way for the Indian military to set up outposts along and over the disputed border. The Indian Army gets deployed to this region and as a result the Chinese Army takes counteractions by setting up their own outposts. This results in off and on skirmishes over the years.

It is October 4, 1968. A 22-year-old Indian Army officer, Captain Harbhajan Singh, is one of many soldiers assigned to fight and defend the border. On this day, the Captain is assigned a mission to transport a convoy of much-needed supplies to a distant outpost where his countrymen lay waiting. In order to avoid enemy detection, the Captain leaves his military post just as the darkness of night approaches. It is cold and raining and the Captain begins marching toward his mission in the dangerous and seemingly changing terrain. The march is long and the terrain makes it even more difficult. The Captain feels thirsty and walks toward the fast-flowing stream. He collects water but right before drinking it, he slips and falls into the river. There is no one to help and soon Captain Singh drowns and dies.

The soldiers of the outpost, anticipating the arrival of the

Captain, send some men to walk along the route to see if the Captain can be seen. When there is no sign of Captain Singh, the soldiers send a radio signal to the command headquarters and a search party is dispatched. Forty-eight hours pass and the search party fails to locate the missing Captain and they return to the base. On that night, the commander of the search party sees a dream wherein Captain Singh appears to him and tells him where his body can be located. In the early hours of the next morning, the commander leads a search party himself and walks to the location he had just seen in his dream. To the surprise of everyone, the body of Captain Singh is located at the exact location seen in the dream. The body is then transported to the military base where it is cremated.

Shortly afterwards, another commander at the military base sees a dream and in the dream, the late Captain Singh tells him that a shrine should be built in his honor at the location where his drowned body was found. The dream is related to the base commanding officer who issues an order that a memorial be built in the honor of the late Captain Harbhajan Singh. The soldiers begin to build a memorial which gradually gets upgraded until it finally turns into a shrine receiving visitors. Inside the shrine is a bedroom with a bathroom attached to it.

Inside the bedroom is a bed with pillows and a military-issue blanket and linen. The uniform of the late Captain hangs from a wall and his Army boots lay nearby. A soldier is assigned who watches over the shrine and is considered as a sort of 'assistant' to the late Captain. The soldier-assistant irons the uniform and shines the medals as well as polishes the boots of the Captain. The soldier-assistant reportedly makes the bed every morning because the bed linen is found 'crumpled.' The soldier-assistant has also been seen polishing the 'muddy' boots of the late Captain every morning. The crumpled bed linen and the muddy boots have been reported by numerous individuals and witnessed by many more. It is reported that the late Captain wears his uniform including boots and patrols the border whence he was once stationed, hence the muddy boots. It is also reported that the late Captain often sleeps at his bed—without anyone seeing him do so—which results in the neatly-made military style bed and linen getting crumpled.

Soldiers stationed at that military base began visiting the shrine and soon the story spread like a wildfire and in a matter of months, soldiers from the surrounding bases also began visiting the shrine. Senior level officers from all branches of the Indian military have also been seen visiting the shrine. It is reported by those who visit the shrine that a cold chill can be felt as well as the presence of an unseen being, which they refer to as 'the spirit of the dead Captain.' The late Captain Singh received a new title, an honorable title, that of a 'Baba.' The visitors state that they derive energy and power from visiting the shrine. Some have reported that the spirit of the Baba alters their mind in order to communicate and give advice.

Reports of unexplained sightings at the border have since increased and it is widely believed, even today, that the sightings are of the spirit of late Captain. Soldiers positioned at the guard towers have reported the presence of the spirit of Baba checking up on them. Sentries at the Line of Control have reported being slapped in the face by an unseen being. The soldiers believe the spirit of the Baba patrols the Line of Control and wakes up the sentries who get sleepy by slapping them, or in some instances, scaring them, which can most definitely take the sleep out of the soldier, making him alert. Reports of the spirit of the Baba are not one-sided. The enemy of the late Captain, the Chinese soldiers have on several occasions complained of *'a man in Indian Army uniform appearing bright and riding a horse'* that patrols the Line of Control and enters the territory of China. The Chinese soldiers follow the man who then suddenly disappears into thin air near the Indian Territory.

The Indian military has not suspended the monthly pay of the late Captain Singh and his salary is still sent to his family. This is due to the popular belief that Captain Singh continues to be a soldier guarding the Indian border. Some individuals have had visions or dreams wherein the spirit of the late Captain appeared to them and conversed with them. These individuals have reported that the spirit notified them saying *'in case of a Chinese aggression or invasion, he [the spirit of Baba] will notify the Indian command up to three days in advance.'*

The late Captain also receives two months of paid leave annually during which his bags are packed and shipped to his house in the state of Punjab, where his family resides. While he is on leave in Punjab, the late Captain's bed linens stay neat and his boots do not get muddy. This has been reported by several individuals, including the soldier-assistant who guards the shrine.

When tensions at the border increase, the Indian and Chinese

Army officers meet at the Line of Control, at the no-man's-land, and this is called a flag meet. During the flag meet talks, the Chinese officers have always brought an extra chair for the spirit of the Baba.

'Spirit of Dead Brother'

In the recent years, many scrolls and diaries have been unearthed from the sites of battles which took place during the First and Second World Wars. Personal diaries written by soldiers who fought in the World Wars describe battlefield encounters with ghosts and spirits witnessed by dozens of soldiers. One such strange encounter occurred to a Canadian soldier in the year 1917, shortly after the Battle of Vimy Ridge. The following is the story of Corporal Will R. Bird.

In the year 1917, Canadian Army Soldier Corporal Will R. Bird served in the 42nd Battalion of the Canadian Black Watch. Two years prior, in 1915, Corporal Will's brother Steve had died fighting in the war. At the battlefield of Vimy Ridge, Corporal Will and two other soldiers lay asleep. Suddenly Corporal Will is awoken by two warm hands touching his back. Corporal Will wakes up to see his dead brother Steve in front of him. Steve leads his brother and they walk through some ruins until they reach the end of the battlefield. There Steve turns a corner and disappears. The sleepy and confused Corporal Will is sure that Steve had died a few years before. Overcome with exhaustion and emotion, Corporal Will settles for sleep at the new location and dismisses the appearance of his brother as an illusion.

Several hours later, Corporal Will wakes up and returns to his post where he finds his post destroyed from an enemy mortar shell and his two fellow soldiers deceased. It is then that Corporal Will is convinced that the spirit of his dead brother Steve returned the previous night to save him.

'City Councilor Takes Photo of Spirit'

On the evening of February 3, 2017, the Councilor for Vegas del Genil City of Granada Province of Spain, was working late at his governmental office when he suddenly felt the air turn cold. The city Councilor stated, *"The air turned abnormally cold in the office so I put on my coat and then got up to go the bathroom [when suddenly] I heard a strange rustling sound in the hallway, as if someone was dragging files across the floor."*

The Councilor became very scared and his first thought was

that there were thieves inside the government building. He quietly walked toward the door but was too afraid to turn on the lights and check the hallway so he froze by the door of his office, which led to the hallway from whence the voices were coming.

The Councilor located his phone and intended to contact the Police Department to report a robbery in progress at the government office but decided to take a photo of the hallway to see if he could spot the supposed thieves. He put his phone on silent and turned off the auto-flash and silently walked toward the hallway to take a photo. Once the photo was taken, the Councilor silently locked himself inside his office and started looking at the picture while listening for any noise coming from the hallway. After an initial glance he was satisfied that no one was at the hallway but a second look at the photo showed what appeared to be a little ghostly-shaped girl standing at the hallway, looking directly toward the Councilor. The terrified Councilor contacted his colleagues and friends for help and sent them the picture he had taken moments earlier.

Shortly afterwards, the Mayor of the city was informed of this incident and initially thought it was a joke. But soon others in the government office complained of *'a sudden change in the temperature where the air turns cold.'* Several officials complained of other unexplainable phenomenon and requested the Mayor to take immediate action. The Mayor's office hired a technician to check the heating system of the office which revealed no abnormalities. But due to the clear appearance of a little girl in the picture, the Mayor has been forced to hire an exorcist who could perform exorcism rituals to get rid of the spirit/ghost of the little girl.

(Photo taken by the City Councilor on February 3, 2017)

'I am Still Alive'

Irfan Mohammad, a 35-year-old man from the village of Jalalpur, India, died as a result of what the family believes was black magic. In March 2016, Irfan was pronounced dead by physicians after being ill for several years. He was buried according to Islamic rituals at the family's private cemetery, twenty feet outside the family house in the village of Jalalpur.

Rizwan, the younger brother of the deceased, stated,

"I spent a lot of time praying at my brother's grave. We believe he died as a result of a black magic spell. Three days after the burial, I was at the grave and I heard singing

coming out of his grave. At first, I thought I was hallucinating but the singing continued. I ran back to my house and notified my father who came to the grave and heard the singing voice coming from my brother's grave."

The news of this strange phenomenon spread fast in the village. Several villagers claim to have heard a voice coming from Irfan's grave saying, *'I am alive, I am still alive, take me out.'* The family of the deceased man has heard the singing over a dozen times. Shortly after this strange phenomenon began, the family filed an excavation petition with the local government. The local magistrate ordered an investigation and the petition to excavate is pending approval.

A group known as the Paranormal Society of India sent investigators to the grave site where they concluded that a paranormal activity is indeed taking place.

'Screaming From the Grave'

In August 2016, Neysi Perez, a 16-year-old female, suddenly collapsed at home. Her parents believed she was being possessed by a demon and called in a priest to perform an exorcism. During the exorcism, the family noticed Neysi foaming at her mouth. She was transported to a local hospital where the physicians pronounced her dead. Neysi was laid in a coffin in her wedding gown, which she had worn only three months prior. She was placed in a concrete tomb at a local cemetery and laid to rest according to Catholic rituals.

A day after the funeral, Neysi's husband Rudy Gonzales went to visit her at the cemetery. While standing by the grave, he began to hear banging and screaming coming out of the grave. Rudy stated,

"As I put my hand on her grave, I could hear noises [coming from] inside. I heard banging, and then I heard Neysi's voice. She was screaming for help. It had already been a day since we [had] buried her. I couldn't believe it. I was ecstatic, full of hope."

Rudy rushed to the cemetery workers and begged them to take his wife out. A cemetery worker also confirmed hearing voices coming from Neysi's grave.

Moments later, the deceased Neysi's family arrived at the cemetery and began breaking the concrete tomb. The family took the coffin out of the tomb and drove to a nearby hospital where doctors began examination.

The primary physician stated,

"The whole family rushed in . . . carrying the girl in her casket. . . . Everybody was claiming she was alive so I went through all the necessary procedures. We evaluated and tried

everything but the girl was dead. They put her back in the coffin and took her away again, back to the cemetery."

'The Jinn-Man Relations'

Historical reports from medieval Europe indicate that Catholic Sisters or Nuns who lived in female-only sanctuaries throughout Europe became pregnant by non-human beings. The Catholic Church later agreed that these children were fathered by the demon. This strange phenomenon is not limited to Catholics or Christians; in fact several people in the Muslim world have also put forward similar claims. Although the Muslim and the Christian call the 'intruding being' by different names, the details of the act and of the intrusion are very similar.

In his informative book titled, *'Ibn Taymeeyah's Essay on the*

Jinn', Dr. Bilal Philips, a highly influential Muslim mind of our times and a well-known speaker and author, writes,

> *"The occasional possession of man [or woman] by the Jinn may be due to sensual desire on the part of the Jinn, capricious whims, or even love, just as it may be among humans. Jinns and humans may also have intercourse with each other and beget children. This is a frequent occurrence which is well known to many."*

Dr. Philips writes from the works of the famous theorist and sociologist Leonard Trelawny Hobhouse and writer Harold T. Christensen that,

> *"Many monks and nuns of medieval Europe reported that they were visited and ravished by voluptuous female demons which were officially called Succubi and equally seductive and alluring fallen angels called Incubi. Subsequently, many nuns became pregnant and killed their children at birth, burying them outside the nunneries."*

In the year 2017, government-appointed investigators located a mass-grave containing the remains of 796 babies at a former Catholic care home in the town of Tuam, Ireland. The home was run by a Catholic religious order of Nuns. Some historians and investigators claim that such mass-graves exist all across Europe dating back to the Medieval Period.

'The Ghost Lovers of Amethyst'

On July 12, 2017, a British woman by the name of Amethyst Realm appeared on the famous British television show 'This Morning' and claimed to have several different ghost lovers. She claimed to have had sexual relations with ghosts for over ten years. Soon all of the major newspapers of Europe and the United States covered her story.

The 27-year-old Amethyst Realm stated,

"It started as an energy, then became physical. There was pressure on my thighs and breath on my neck. . . . I had sex with the ghost. You can feel it. It's difficult to explain.

There was a weight and a weightlessness, a physical breath and stroking, and the energy as well. [I] could feel the connection."

Amethyst stated that the sexual relations with the first ghost continued for nearly three years but it had to be ended because her human fiancée caught her cheating with the ghost. She stated,

> *"He [the fiancé] came home from work a day early . . . and he says [that] he saw a [shadowy] shape of a man through the spare room window when he pulled up [to the house]."*

After the first relationship ended, Amethyst began receiving other visitors from the ghosts and spirits. She stated,

> *"[I] can always feel the difference - the same with humans, I guess - you can just feel different presences. It is often different ones. . . . I have got no interest in men now."*

Amethyst was asked if there was a possibility that she imagined it all or that she dreamt it or had a sort of sleep paralysis. She responded,

> *"I do not think so because my first ghost used to follow*

me around the house and kind of lure me in so I was definitely awake while walking around. . . . I would like to find one to settle down with and spend the rest of my life with."

Amethyst stated she has been researching into phantom pregnancies and wants to become pregnant by the ghost and have a ghost child.

'The 100-Year-Old Ghost Lover'

A British woman from the County of Shropshire, United Kingdom, known as Sian Jameson, recently claimed to have had the *'best sexual relations'* with a ghost who had lived over 100 years ago. Sian stated that she moved into a new apartment which had many books and paintings. One particular ancient painting hanging on the wall of her bedroom was of a man named Robert, *'a handsome man with dark hair, wearing a white shirt.'* After a few months of living at the new apartment, one day Sian was visited by a ghost.

Sian Jameson, the 26-year-old British woman, stated, *"I woke up early one morning to find a dark-haired, very good-looking young man lying next to me. He was fully clothed, in a loose white shirt. . . . I told myself I was dreaming and rolled away from him. As I faced the wall, I slowly realized I wasn't asleep and, suddenly I was frozen with fear. I felt a hand on my waist but the touch was strange—light and cool. . . . His body was soft and light . . . he felt almost weightless. . . . [It was Robert, the ghost of the man who had lived 100 years ago]."*

Sian stated she recognized the ghost as Robert from the old painting hanging on her wall. She said after the sexual relations, the ghost disappeared, leaving her wondering if any of it was real. She concluded that she had a vivid dream. But then, a few days later, the ghost returned. Sian stated,

> *"Again, he appeared in the morning and . . . [after sexual relations I watched him] leave the room. I was expecting to hear his footsteps on the wooden stairs, but there was no sound."*

Sian claims that the ghost came to visit her again for the third time and that after that evening, she fell in love with him.

Many other individuals, including many celebrities, have

claimed to have had similar interactions with the so-called spirits and ghosts. Recently, the famous American singer and actor Bobby Brown claimed that he was visited by a ghost who had sexual relations with him at his mansion in the US state of Georgia.

'The Jinn or Dead Spirits'

In the recent years, the so-called medium community has witnessed publicity in a manner unprecedented in history. Mediums who claim to be able to speak with the spirits of the deceased are appearing daily on radio and television shows. They appear in reality shows as well as the news channels to perform live readings. During the shows, an individual or a group from the audience volunteers for a reading, and the medium then calls on and converses with the deceased family or friends of the volunteer live on television. In most cases a microphone is provided to the volunteer so that he/she can concur or point out the mistakes of the medium, which rarely happens. During the live readings, the medium shares with the volunteer details about the deceased person, such as his/her name, type of death and often such details that only a close family or friend would know.

There are various ways through which the mediums claim to receive information from the spirit of the dead. Recently a medium explained the different methods of channeling to me as follows,

Clairsentience, meaning Clear-Feeling: During this session, the medium feels the same physical ailment as the spirit of the deceased person before its death and passes along the complaint.

Clairalience, meaning Clear-Smelling: During this session, the medium is able to receive information by smelling the spirit of the deceased person and collecting information such as but not limited to the scent of smoking, alcohol, and blood.

Clairgustance, meaning Clear-Tasting: This is similar to Clairalience 'Clear-Smelling' but via the ability to taste.

Clairaudience, meaning Clear-Hearing: During this session, the medium is able to hear the voice and thoughts of the spirit of the deceased person. Some mediums claim to have the ability to hear the spirits just as they are able to hear normal human voices, while others claim that the voice of the spirit enters the mind and they cannot truly hear it in the normal sense.

Clairvoyance, meaning Clear-Seeing: During this session, the medium is able to see things normal humans cannot, such as the ability to see the spirits of the deceased roaming all around us. Similar to Clairaudience, 'Clear-Hearing', some mediums claim to have the ability to actually see the spirits, while others see images in their mind provided by the spirit of the deceased.

In the ancient books, they are recorded as witches and fortune tellers who are helped by the Jinn. In our times, they are known by various names such as crystal-gazers, psychics, spiritualists, clairvoyants, a telepath, mind-reader or a medium. Amongst them are those who call themselves magicians and those practicing black magic. These are some of the many fancy names attributed to them. In recent years, several modern types have also emerged. The modern types use technological equipment such as radios and computers and other electronic equipment to capture the voices of the spirits and to converse with them. Although many of these individuals have been proven as frauds and tricksters, there are many amongst them who are able to accomplish or perform paranormal activities such as moving objects without touching them, or the ability to provide personal details about a deceased person known only to a close family member, the ability to provide information on lost objects and/or assistance in murder cases and child abduction cases. In the following pages, I will try and describe some of their paranormal activities.

'The Young Couple in Arizona'

I personally know a young couple who reside in the state of Arizona, United States, who had a strange experience with a psychic by the name of John. I am well acquainted with the trustworthy couple and I will write their story just as it was narrated to me by the husband, who stated,

"My wife was very close to her grandmother so when she passed away my wife became depressed. She stopped going to work and avoided food and drink. She would not communicate with me. She became very depressed and I decided to seek help. This person so and so whom I knew told me about a secret psychic by the name of John and asked me to contact him at a time when my wife would be present with me.

He told me that John would say things to comfort my wife. I agreed and went home, where I found my wife lying on her bed. Without consulting her, I pulled out my cell phone and contacted John, who answered his phone. I told him who I was and how I came across his phone number. I told John that I was going to put him on speaker phone so that my wife could hear what he had to say. Up until that moment, even I did not know what John was going to say. Then John began asking questions such as the name of my wife and the name of her deceased grandmother. After a short silent pause, John's voice started to change. It was still a man's voice but different from the earlier voice. The new voice stated,

'Sallam so and so . . . [My wife's name] I want you to know that I am here for you. I want you to not be sad, for I am not dead. My spirit is alive and I continue to watch over you. I want you to resume speaking with your husband. I want you to start eating again, for it is not right . . . it is really not right for a pregnant woman to stay hungry. I have left some gold bracelets for you behind the cabinet in my room. I want you to keep some of them and send some to your cousins in Afghanistan. I want you to know that I will always be watching over you.'

"When I heard John say my wife is pregnant, I thought

to myself this idiot is going way too far and that he is a liar. I continued to think that this man was lying but I did not say anything to my wife because it was I who had initiated this session. But then I saw my wife sit upright and weep. After John got off the phone, my wife began to cry even more. Later, she told me that John was right and that she indeed had cousins living in Kabul, Afghanistan. That same evening, my wife and I drove to the deceased grandmother's house, wherein my wife found the gold bracelets wrapped in a small handkerchief behind the cabinet. That same evening, my wife took an at-home pregnancy test and indeed she was pregnant. Up until that moment, we did not know of my wife's pregnancy. After that day, my wife acted like her normal self."

'The Story of Shaykh Ahmad Izz ad-Deen'

Shaykh Ahmad Izz ad-Deen is the author of the outstanding book titled, *'Al-Eemaan bil Malaaikah'*, translated into English as 'Belief in the Angels.' The writer was introduced to and met with a Muslim medium who was able to speak with the spirit of the deceased, but not just any deceased individual. This medium was able to invite and, through channeling, converse with the spirits of the noble Companions of the Honorable Prophet Muhammad, such as the spirit of the Companion Abu Hurrayra, and the spirits of deceased Islamic scholars, theologians and jurists. The complete story is mentioned in his book titled above. Here I will provide a short version,

"I met a man who claimed that he used the Jinn to do good things to help people, by means of a human medium. . . . The medium came to me one day and told me that I had been invited by a male and a female [from amongst] the Jinn, to discuss a matter which would be in my best interest. So I went at the appointed time, putting my trust in the Almighty God. . . I entered the house of the medium, and we sat together in a room, where he sat on a bed. We started—under his direction of course—to recite prayers for forgiveness . . . until he [the medium] fell into a trance. I laid him down on his bed and covered him with a blanket, as he had told me to do. Then in a low voice, his friend from amongst the Jinn greeted me and expressed his joy at meeting me and his love for me. He introduced himself and told me that he was a created being, claiming that he was neither an Angel nor a Jinn, but another kind of creature which came into existence by the Word of the

Almighty God, 'Be!' and he was. According to his [the being speaking through the medium] claims, the Jinn followed the instructions of no one but himself, and that there were only five mediums between him and the Almighty God, the fifth of whom was the Archangel Gabriel. He started praising me, saying that they would cut off all other ties with mankind and be content with meeting me only, because I was the special person of this era—or so he claimed—a person who was under the special care of the Almighty God, and the Almighty God was the One Who had chosen me for that. He made amazing promises to me, promises that were astounding. . . . When the first meeting ended, he invited me to another meeting on another occasion; then he himself taught me a special recitation to awaken him from his trance. This was done and the medium sat up and rubbed his eyes as if he was waking up from a deep sleep and did not know what had been happening. I went back to the next appointment as well, and we met for a long time on each occasion after that. In every meeting the wonderful promises were repeated. . . . The matter went further. Many spirits started to visit me at every meeting . . . I would be with the medium eating food or having a cup of tea, and he would fall into his usual trance and tilt his head forward until it rested on his chest, then the visitor who claimed to be an Angel or Jinn .

. . would talk to me, showing a great deal of respect, saying that he [the spirit visitor] was being blessed by his visit with me and giving me glad tidings of a prosperous and blessed future. Then he would go away, and another one would come, and another. . . . Individuals from amongst the Angels visited me and individuals from amongst the Jinn, and Abu Hurrayra [a Companion of the Honorable Prophet Muhammad] from amongst the Companions . . . as well as some scholars and virtuous people whom I had met and who had died . . . they gave me the glad tidings that my father would visit me at a time set by them. I looked forward to the visit anxiously. When the time came, they asked me to recite Surah al-Waaqiyah [The 56th Chapter of the Quran] aloud, and I read it. When I finished reading it, they said, 'your father will come after a few moments; listen to what he says but do not ask him anything!' After a few moments . . . the one who they claimed was my father came to me and greeted me, expressing his happiness at meeting me and his joy over my contact with these spirits. He advised me to take care of the medium and his family, and to look after him with compassion and kindness . . . [then the spirit of the deceased father] ended his speech with As-Sallah al-Ibraheemiyah [the prayer of Prophet Abraham]. I knew that he [my deceased father] used to love very much to send

blessing upon the Prophet, especially the Sallah al Ibraheemiyah. What was amazing was that the tone of voice and accent of the one who spoke to me was to some extent similar to my father's tone of voice and accent. Then he said Sallam and left. I started to wonder, why did they tell me not to ask him anything? There was definitely something strange behind this! The reason behind it dawned on me at that point: this was not my father; it was his 'Qareen' [Companion from amongst the Jinn] who had accompanied him all his life. He had come to me in my father's form, imitating some of his characteristics. They told me not to ask him anything because the Qareen is one of the Jinn, and no matter what he knew about my father and his circumstances, he could not know every little thing that a son would know about his father. So they were afraid that I might ask him about something and he would not be able to answer, and thus their deceit would be exposed.'

It is narrated in the Books of Hadith (Sayings and Teachings of the Prophet) that the Honorable Prophet Muhammad stated,

> *"There is none of you who does not have a Qareen [Companion] appointed for him from amongst the Jinn."*

When the Companions asked, *"Even you, O Prophet of God?"*

The Honorable Prophet replied, *"Even me, but the Almighty God has helped me against him...."*

'Amelie Van Tass Assisted by the Jinn'

Amelie Van Tass is an Austrian woman who along with her fiancée are known as The Clairvoyants. The couple became famous after performing live readings on several shows including the well-known America's Got Talent television show. After several live performances, The Clairvoyants reached second place in the America's Got Talent show.

During an interview, Amelie stated that as a young girl, she had a feeling that she was different from other people; however, she did not know what that difference was, but knew that it existed.

Years later, Amelie met a man by the name of Thommy Ten and they started a relationship. Amelie stated that she knew there was a special connection between the two as soon as they had met. One day whilst in a different city, Thommy contacted Amelie by phone and she asked him a strange question. Amelie asked if Thommy was holding a rose in his hand. Thommy was shocked and inquired as to how she knew there was a rose in his hand. Amelie could not explain how she knew except that she did. Shortly afterwards, the couple realized that Amelie was able to see in her mind's eye everything that Thommy touched or held.

While blindfolded Amelie can correctly guess anything Thommy holds in his hand and in some cases, anything Thommy sees. During a live television show, a one-hundred-dollar bill was taken from the pocket of an individual, and the blindfolded Amelie was able to correctly read the serial number of the hundred-dollar bill. There are claims that Amelie is able to see things Thommy holds even when they are in separate areas.

Amelie claims to be the only living female Clairvoyant in the world. Many have concluded that Amelie is being assisted by the Jinn, who whisper the answers to her.

'Government Use of Psychics'

Recently declassified documents show that the United States government officials have used psychics for reasons ranging from checking on the conditions of the Americans held hostage in Iran to getting updates on the former Soviet Union Navy's submarines. In the years 2016 and 2017, the Central Intelligence Agency (CIA) released several previously classified documents which clearly show the extent of government-hired psychics. In 1970s, the US intelligence agencies and military began recruiting and training psychics for the purpose of collecting intelligence which operatives in the field could not get their hands on and intelligence satellites could not capture. To go places without actually going there!

How? By using Extra Sensory Perception (ESP) and other methods. Some historians have claimed that the government had been involved in similar projects even in the 1940s and 1950s. Records indicate that during World War II, the Nazi party was working on psychic projects as well as black magic and that they searched for ancient scrolls and books which contained information on black magic. After the defeat of the Nazi party, the United States and Soviet Union collected the works of the Nazis and built on it. Here are some examples of the US government's use of psychics who in truth have no special psychic abilities and are being assisted by the Jinn who gather and whisper partial information to them.

In the year 1958, the American nuclear submarine USS Nautilus became the first vessel to reach the North Pole by travelling under ice caps. American sailors onboard the submarine were attempting to send a 'mission achieved' message to a US government facility thousands of miles away in the state of Maryland, where a 'human-receiver/psychic' awaited. The sailors were not using any type of electronics to send the message but instead by psychic methods such as ESP. It was reported that one US sailor was successful in sending the message using black and white cards with images.

THE WORLD *of* THE UNSEEN

In the year 1970, an ex-Israeli soldier by the name of Uri Geller popularized ESP. He claimed he was able to see inside sealed containers, read people's minds and bend spoons using only his mind. He performed these acts in private as well as on television shows. A few years later, the CIA and the Stanford Research Institute conducted several experiments on Uri Geller. Around the same time, a Soviet woman by the name of Ninel Kulagina became famous for being able to move objects using her mind. She also performed on a television show, leaving observers shocked.

One of the longest of these experiments was the US government funded project known as 'The Remote Viewing Program.' A psychic, also known as a 'Remote Viewer', would sit in a windowless room and see events thousands of miles away. The government even carried out experiments to train and develop and turn normal individuals into 'Remote Viewers.' Most of these programs were concentrated on collecting intelligence which again operatives in the field could not get their hands on and satellites could not capture.

In the year 1979, Iranian Revolutionaries suddenly stormed the

American Embassy in Iran and held 52 Americans as hostages for a total of 444 days. Recently declassified records show that the US Joint Chiefs of Staff—the highest ranking member from each branch of the US military—sought help from the Remote Viewers. During that time, the psychics revealed information such as the location of the hostages and the conditions and the type of uniforms the guards wore. The psychics even stated that one of the hostages was in a poor mental state and suffered from Multiple Sclerosis. All of the information turned out to be correct.

In the year 1981, United States Army Brigadier General James Dozier was kidnapped in Italy by members of the organization known as the Red Brigades. The US Government used all of its usual methods but could not locate the kidnapped General. Then the US Government sought help from some Remote Viewers. The Remote Viewers worked as a psychic unit run by the US Army under Project GRILL-FLAME. A psychic known as Joe McMoneagle located the room where the kidnapped General was being held. Joe told the investigators that the General was held at a house and chained to a wall heater in the City of Padua, Italy. Later the General was released in the City of Padua, Italy.

Another similar story occurred in the year 1988, when United States marine Colonel William Higgins was kidnapped by the group known as the Hezbollah. The US Government sought help from the Remote Viewers. One of the psychics known as Angela Dellafiora told investigators—amongst other things—that the Colonel was being 'held on water' and pointed on a map to a location in Lebanon. Later, it was discovered that the Colonel had been killed in Lebanon and that his body was kept on ice.

The US government-funded program known as Project STARGATE is one of many government-funded projects dealing with psychics and mediums. Project STARGATE was run by the CIA and the Stanford Research Institute, both of whom conducted several experiments to see if psychic abilities could be performed under strictly controlled environments and on command. In August of 1973, the ex-Israeli soldier, psychic and spoon-bender Uri Geller took part in an eight-day experiment. During the test, researchers from the CIA and Stanford Research Institute asked Uri Geller to duplicate images and drawings that were produced by a researcher in a different windowless room whom Geller could not hear nor see. The controlled image drawn by the researcher in the windowless room was of a 'bunch of grapes—24 grapes to be exact.' Then later in a controlled room, Uri Geller began drawing a bunch with 24 grapes in it, shocking all of the government observers. CIA observers wrote that in this experiment and others 'Uri Geller's psychic abilities were convincing.'

As stated previously, in each and every one of these cases, the Jinn are involved and these are not special psychic abilities but the tricks of the Jinnkind.

PART 4

'Exorcism and Exorcists'

Exorcism is the ritual by which demons or Jinns are taken out of a possessed human's body. Exorcisms are performed by Jews, Christians and Muslims alike. Although each group conducts the ritual differently, the purpose and goals are the same. Some expel the Jinn by reciting verses from the Holy Scriptures like the Holy Torah, the Holy Gospels and the Glorious Quran, while others sweet-talk the Jinn into leaving the body of the possessed human. There are even those who threaten the possessing Jinn by sending after him/her much stronger Jinns. I know of a person who performs exorcisms on possessed

Muslims and those of other faiths and his technique is to threaten the Jinn, saying, *'Depart or I shall send after you my Jinn who is stronger than you; depart or I shall send my Jinn after your family.'* Obviously, such exorcisms are not supported by Orthodox Islam or even by Christianity or Judaism.

As I have already stated in the previous pages, I am no scholar and I have no special abilities. I cannot recommend a particular technique or verses of the Holy Books of the Almighty God to be used during an exorcism. That is the duty of the scholars and men of knowledge and they have already performed their duties to the best of their abilities. Their outstanding books such as the works of the great Islamic scholars Ibn Taymeeyah, Ibn Hanbal, Al-Shafi'i, Al-Bayhaqi and Al-Asqalani amongst other Muslim scholars, and the works of men of knowledge of our times such as Umar Al-Ashqaar, Ahmad Sakr and Dr. Bilal Philips are out there for the seeker of knowledge.

However, I can state with full confidence how an exorcism should not be performed and which type of exorcists must be avoided. Any types of exorcism and healings which go against the Glorious Quran and the Holy Scriptures and the ways of the Honorable Prophets must be avoided, regardless of how pious and knowledgeable the exorcist may seem and regardless of his/her success rate.

The following are a few examples of exorcisms which are prohibited by both the Glorious Quran and the Holy Bible and must be avoided at any cost.

'Blowing the Holy Spirit'

Around the year 2008, an American woman from the state of Virginia filled a lawsuit in US Court against an exorcist. The woman, who chose to remain anonymous and was hence known only as 'Jane Doe', stated that she believed she was possessed by the demons and decided to seek help from a Catholic Church.

Reverend Thomas Euteneuer is a famous Catholic priest and the Director of one the largest anti-abortion groups in the US.

He is famous for his television speeches and considered one of the best in his field.

The possessed woman, Jane Doe, met with the Reverend in the year 2008 and in the meetings which followed, the Reverend told Miss Doe that she was possessed by evil spirits. The Reverend agreed to help her. Miss Doe met with the Reverend several times in his office and in other locations. During the exorcism sessions, the Reverend would sprinkle holy water and say prayers.

The Reverend Thomas Euteneuer would then,

"Kiss the corners of her mouth and stroke her legs, breasts and thighs; caressed her face; laid his body on top of hers; and frequently explained full, passionate kisses as 'blowing the Holy Spirit into her.'"

Miss Doe claims that on one occasion, the Reverend called her to his hotel room in order to pray on her and remove the evil spirits. In the hotel, the Reverend told her to remove her clothes and assaulted her.

'I Give You the Power'

There is a Muslim Babaji [saint, mystic] in India by the name of Baba Razaullah. The Baba, an elderly man, claims to have given power to the roaming souls of thousands of unjustly killed individuals, so that they may seek justice.

According to the Baba,

> *"The spirit or soul of a person who commits suicide as well as those murdered or unjustly killed roams around the Earth after the body dies. This unjustly killed soul roams around seeking justice but is unable to do so. I am able to give the souls power to attain justice."*

The Baba claims to have the ability to speak with the deceased person's soul through his/her family. The Baba states,

> *"If the person was murdered by someone, I summon the soul of the deceased to enter the body of and speak through the mouth of his family member. Then I ask the soul questions such as who killed him and the reason for the killing. Then if I see*

that the soul is truthful and was unjustly killed, I give him the power and the ability to go after the murderer and attain justice."

According to the Baba, he gives power to the soul to go after not only the murderer, but also the murderer's offspring. If a man was pushed from the top of a building, the Baba gives his soul to power to go after the murderer to push him from a building and to do the same to his family.

If the soul lies while communicating with the Baba, then the Baba possesses the ability to *"cut the soul in two, burn the soul and send it to the Hereafter."* Amazingly, each time the Baba 'sends' a soul to the Hereafter, he says to it, *"Insha-Allah [God-Willing], now I give you the power to go the Hereafter."* The Baba starts each session by reciting verses from the Glorious Quran.

The Baba and the thousands of individuals who seek his help are deaf, blind and heedless to the verses of the Glorious Quran wherein the Almighty God says,

"From the Earth We created you, and into it We will return you, and from it We will extract you another time." **The Quran: Ch. 20 - V. 55.**

"And they ask you about the soul. Say, the soul is of the affair of my Lord. And mankind have not been given of knowledge except a little." **The Quran: Ch. 17 - V. 85.**

PART 5

'Conclusion'

I have always been certain of the existence of the Jinnkind and now, after several years of research, my certainty has only increased. During my research I came across many other 'characters' such as magicians who practice white magic and those involved in black magic and others whose stories were rare and interesting. I also heard of and/or witnessed individuals who dealt with the Jinnkind and many others who were possessed or formerly possessed by the Jinn. Their stories were eye-opening. I wish I had the time and the resources to share all of those stories. The belief in the existence of Jinnkind is important, for they live on Earth as our neighbors and are part of our lives, but in the Hereafter no individual will be questioned on the existence of the Jinn. As humans, we should know who the Jinnkind are and what they usually do and how they usually do those things so that we could protect ourselves from the evil ones amongst them. However, we must not go after them in order to try and utilize them. Some people say they utilize the Jinnkind in order to do good for Mankind. This is not a correct way of thinking, for good can only come from and with the permission of the Almighty God.

As humans, we are not 'way too smart' for the Jinns, as some individuals have claimed. An individual dealing with the Jinnkind may think he is controlling the Jinn, but in reality it is the opposite and the Jinn is probably controlling him. Our Father Adam and Mother Eve were not 'way too smart' when they chose to believe the whispers of Satan, the evil one from the Jinnkind, so how can we as children of Adam and Eve claim to be 'way too smart' for the Jinnkind?

During my research I always tried my best to gather accurate information. I am not a GEN-ius and I am most certainly not being assisted by my GEN-ius or Jinn companion. This is the best I was able to do. And the Almighty God knows best.

I affirm that there is no one worthy of worship except the Almighty God Who is the Creator of the Heavens and the Earth and everything in between, and I affirm my belief in His Angels and Prophets and Books.

THE WORLD *of* THE UNSEEN

'Notes'

www.ingramcontent.com/pod-product-compliance
Lightning Source LLC
Chambersburg PA
CBHW020230170426
43201CB00007B/378